C000177573

# THE BLACKBIRD'S NEST

# The Blackbird's Nest

*An Anthology of Poetry*
*from Queen's University Belfast*

*edited by*
FRANK ORMSBY

*foreword by*
SEAMUS HEANEY

*afterword by*
CIARAN CARSON

THE
BLACKSTAFF
PRESS

BELFAST

QUEEN'S UNIVERSITY BELFAST
IN ASSOCIATION WITH THE SEAMUS HEANEY CENTRE FOR POETRY

The Seamus Heaney Centre for Poetry was established in 2003.
An international base for research and creative writing with a particular
focus on poetry in modern Ireland, the Centre aims to preserve and
enhance the creative and critical tradition of
Queen's University Belfast.

www.qub.ac.uk/heaneycentre

The publication of this anthology was made possible by the
generosity of the following benefactors

Jim and Alice Fitzpatrick

The Queen's University of Belfast Foundation

The Queen's University of Belfast Foundation is an independent,
international body established to advance the strategic goals and
objectives of Queen's University Belfast. Its primary function is
to generate financial support for capital development plans and
academic initiatives.

www.qub.ac.uk/alumni/foundationboard

# CONTENTS

# FOREWORD

$F$rank Ormsby's introduction to this anthology provides a condensed history of the activities and fortunes of poets and poetry in and around Queen's University Belfast. It is a story that begins with no immediate promise but then, as often happens in the creative course of things, it comes quickly to life, burgeons into a narrative full of significant characters and episodes, and develops in the end into an action which 'flared brilliantly ... and was seen by observers far beyond the confines of Northern Ireland'.

That image of literary history as a cometary phenomenon was first used by Norman Dugdale to describe the activity and reputation of the Group organised by Philip Hobsbaum during his time as a lecturer in the English Department in the 1960s, but it applies equally to the overall situation represented in the following pages. For a long time, the poetic light that shone over University Road and environs was fitful, but from the 1940s onwards it gradually strengthened and steadied: the omens were good and the outcome gratifying. Nowadays it would be impossible to make the charge made by John Hewitt in 1945, when he claimed that writers around Queen's had 'produced little work of significance': on the contrary, when Queen's is mentioned in literary company these days, people tend to think of whole constellations of talent, new stars in the poetic firmament, 'new weather' in the province of culture.

Not I, said D.H. Lawrence, but the wind that blows through me. And that is what the Queen's experience offered many. An opportunity to open up to further experience through further language. To begin to realise, through the recognition of peers and professors, that we 'lived in important places'. In my own case, the debt of gratitude has been mounting for a lifetime, from the moment when Donatus Nwoga chose to publish my first poems in the English Department's magazine *Gorgon*, the moment when Denis Tuohy performed a like service in *Q*, the moment when Philip Hobsbaum's Group provided the context and encouragement for a deeper commitment, and that moment years later when it all culminated in honour and the University opened its own Centre for Poetry in my name.

A university is, among other things, a milieu where the speaker of the vernacular encounters and is required to master the *lingua franca* – or perhaps that should be the plural *linguae francae* – and for a poet especially, this has vital consequences. I myself arrived in Queen's with my south Derry accent intact – my 'pushed' and 'pulled' rhyming perfectly with 'hushed and lulled' in the poem Denis Tuohy published in that issue of *Q*. In my sixth form year, I had attained a certain familiarity with the idiom of Milton, but my first speech was closer to that of W.F. Marshall, and I was well versed in his work, knowing by heart a recitation like 'Me and My Da', and knowing (from observation, of course, not from experience) what it meant to be 'in clabber to the knee'. So I could say that whereas for Patrick Kavanagh 'the god of imagination' woke once upon a time 'in a Mucker fog', for me that same god rose in all his mystery out of mid-Ulster clabber. And something similar happened in the life and work of many other poets in the anthology. One of Cathal Ó Searcaigh's poems, for example, returns 'clabber' to its origins in Irish only to take it on a European tour through Rimbaud's Charleville; and Paul Muldoon imagines a way of escaping the muck of local violence by reimagining that legendary 'Truce' in the mud and blood of Flanders. Imagination, in other words, is in constant negotiation between the parish and the universe (as Kavanagh also expressed it) and such negotiation will often have its beginnings in a university education.

Wallace Stevens, a poet more noted for the sumptuous line than the simple statement, once said in the plainest of terms that the function of poetry was to help people live their lives. In different ways, the work included here has done that, and many of the poets have been rewarded with wide publication, critical recognition and a certain local hero(ine) status. Such recognition is good both for the art and the artist, but even so, the true work of poets is done in the quieter reaches of individual consciousness. Their melodies are best heard where Yeats once heard the waves of Lough Gill, 'in the deep heart's core', and readers of *The Blackbird's Nest* will have the opportunity to attend in this most desirable way: they will be able to 'read into themselves'.

The majority of contributors to the anthology were born in Northern Ireland, but many others arrived in the course of a professional life and became part of the ongoing to-and-fro, come-and-go, ebb-and-flow that always characterises a vital artistic milieu. All, however, made something of the place and of their place in it. In an area where politics were contentious and the cultural and constitutional understanding of things contrary, they neither buried their heads nor shot their mouths off. As I read their names on the contents page, I see them lined up, feet on the ground, weather eye open, waiting for the given note and the utterly persuasive work.

But when I remember the title of the book, I also see them as a nestful of 'scaldies', fledglings with their beaks wide open and their wings widely stretched, singers still holding the note first uttered by the Lagan blackbird in the ninth-century Irish poem; I see them as whin-boys and gorse-*girshigh*, Waddell *puellae* and world poets, heirs of that local master who once practised his art with such immediacy and exactitude on the edge of Belfast Lough more than a thousand years ago.

SEAMUS HEANEY

# INTRODUCTION

It is generally accepted that the earliest reference to the
Belfast area in Irish poetry is a doodle by a ninth-century
scribe, possibly a monk, in the margin of the text he was
transcribing. His spirits are lifted by the singing of a
blackbird across the nearby lough and he records the
moment in a short, joyful flourish. The blackbird of
Belfast Lough, as it is sometimes referred to, has become
an iconic presence in poetry from the north of Ireland.
The original poem has been translated from the Irish by
John Montague, Seamus Heaney, Tom Paulin and Ciaran
Carson, among others, and the bird's song also echoes
through poems by John Hewitt and Paul Muldoon. When
the Seamus Heaney Centre for Poetry opened at Queen's
University Belfast in 2003, the blackbird was, fittingly,
adopted as its logo and it seemed appropriate to give it
another symbolic outing in the title of the present
anthology.

The University has not always been so hospitable to
poets and poetry. In 1945, Queen's centenary year, John
Hewitt published an article entitled 'The Bitter Gourd:
Some Problems of the Ulster Writer', in which he

identified as one of the problems 'the part played by [Queen's] in our corporate life'. It had, he argued, 'remained culturally a foreign oasis to us'; creative effort had been 'allowed to go its own way unregarded' and although the University had had literary groups from time to time they had 'produced little work of significance'. Hewitt quotes W.R. Rodgers' description of himself in the preface to *Awake and Other Poems* (1941) as 'schooled in a backwater of literature, out of sight of the running stream of contemporary verse' and declares that it is 'symbolic of the whole context that W.R. Rodgers was not in his university days a practising poet at all'.

Hewitt's strictures are essentially accurate. In its first fifty years the University produced no poets of note. The significant northern poets of the later nineteenth century flourished elsewhere, Sir Samuel Ferguson (1810–86) and Thomas Caulfield Irwin (1823–92) in Dublin and William Allingham (1824–89) in London. The poets associated with the Ulster Literary Theatre in the early twentieth century, such as George Russell (AE), Joseph Campbell, James H. Cousins and Alice Milligan, had no direct connection with Queen's, although the scholar and translator of Chinese and Latin poetry, Helen Waddell, whose brother Samuel Waddell (writing as 'Rutherford Mayne') was a prominent playwright of the period, and who herself wrote a play for the movement, may be said to have had a foot in both camps.

In view of the comments quoted above, it is ironic that John Hewitt and W.R. Rodgers, who had been contemporaries at Queen's during the late 1920s, were among the first graduates to gain a reputation as poets, although they did not publish in book form until the 1940s. This was also the decade during which the university magazine *The Northman* became a platform for emerging undergraduate poets such as Roy McFadden and Robert Greacen, as well as older figures such as Hewitt and Rodgers and prose writers such as Michael McLaverty, John Boyd (both graduates of Queen's) and Sam Hanna Bell. In his autobiography *Even Without Irene* Robert Greacen records how he and others set out to make *The Northman* into 'a journal of reasonable literary quality – "Ulster's only literary magazine" as we called it in showcards displayed by local booksellers' and how they opened its pages to the work of English poets such as Henry Treece and Alex Comfort.

Although the flurry of activity in the 1940s had strong links with the University, the emergence and development of the leading poets of that generation was not actively fostered by Queen's as an institution. The 1960s, however, proved a pivotal decade in this respect. In 1962 the poet Philip Hobsbaum joined the English Department and began a search for local creative talent around which he might build a writers' group similar to one he had previously co-founded in London. Some of the talent was already in waiting. Seamus Heaney, for example, had just graduated and was beginning to publish poems in periodicals outside the University, Stewart Parker was a postgraduate student in the English Department, James Simmons was teaching at Friends' School, Lisburn, and Bernard MacLaverty was working as a laboratory technician in the Queen's Anatomy Department. The

'Belfast Group', as it came to be known, had its first meeting in Hobsbaum's flat in Fitzwilliam Street in the autumn of 1963 and continued to meet there weekly during term time until 1966. In addition to the writers already mentioned, the early membership included Edna Longley (neé Broderick), Arthur Terry, Joan Newmann (neé Watton), Marie Heaney (neé Devlin) and Harry Chambers. The Group quickly expanded to include Michael Longley (who had recently graduated from Trinity College Dublin), Norman Dugdale, John Harvey, Michael Allen and Jack Pakenham, better known as a painter. When Hobsbaum left Belfast in 1966, the Group meetings continued, first in the English Department, then in the Heaneys' house in Ashley Avenue and occasionally in the Four-in-hand pub (now Ryan's) on the Lisburn Road. By the end of the decade its membership included some leading figures from the next generation of Queen's poets, such as Paul Muldoon and Ciaran Carson.

In its original incarnation, the Group speedily became the main focus of literary creativity in Belfast, nurturing emergent talents from widely different backgrounds and from both inside and outside the University. At each meeting a nominated writer would read new work which had previously been circulated to the other members and a critical discussion would follow. Literary friendships and productive rivalries developed and a number of poets progressed towards the pamphlet- and book-length collections that would make the north of Ireland one of the power points of Irish poetry and of poetry in English in the second half of the twentieth century.

Since its demise in the early 1970s, the impact of the Belfast Group has been explored and re-explored, assessed and re-assessed by a range of its members, sometimes with reservations. Seamus Heaney, for example, has paid tribute to Hobsbaum's 'energy, generosity, belief in the community, trust in the parochial, the inept, the unprinted' and credits him with giving 'a generation a sense of themselves', helping to transform them from 'craven provincials' to 'genuine parochials'. For him the Group meetings 'ratified the activity of writing for all of us who shared it'. Michael Longley has described himself as 'taken aback' by Hobsbaum's hostile reaction to his first poems but also as 'stimulated'; he concedes that 'Hobsbaum committed himself to Belfast and the writers there with great energy and generosity', but has stated that he 'didn't alter one semi-colon as a result of Group discussion'. James Simmons acknowledges in a symposium on the Group that he was glad to have 'some serious people paying attention to his work' and, in a letter, describes Hobsbaum as an 'enthusiastic facilitator', adding 'I have seldom felt so like a real poet since I was at Leeds [University]'. In a later autobiographical essay, however, he writes that 'the famous workshop had no effect on my work because I had been at Leeds with equal or superior talents' and claims to remember with more enthusiasm 'the burgeoning folk scene' in Belfast at that time. Stewart Parker, writing in 1976, is more acerbically dismissive, seeming to imply that the whole experience of the Group had made him allergic to contemporary poetry and stating that he has more vivid memories of the New

Stage Club. Arthur Terry counts among the strengths of the Group a 'continuing dialogue of people who were prepared to discuss one another's writing critically ... the attention given to the sound of a poem ... and to the details of its verbal texture', while noting also 'a tendency to overrate ... the dramatic monologue' and 'the auto-biographical lyric' and to attach too much importance to 'subject' and 'theme'. Jack Pakenham found the discussions 'intellectually stimulating' but complains of 'too many academics with identical poetic tastes' and about the repetitive and limited nature of the subjects: 'A bird-watching botanist with a classical education and a mad uncle who loved stoats would have been the ultimate hero in the ultimate poem in this climate.' Derek Mahon, who had little direct connection with the Group, comments on its immediate effect as 'probably first to crystallise the sense of a new Northern poetry' and Norman Dugdale sums up its broader impact when he characterises it as 'a comet with a long tail, that flared brilliantly for a while and was seen by observers far beyond the confines of Northern Ireland'.

The birth of Hobsbaum's Group in the early 1960s coincided with the beginnings of the Queen's University Festival (now the Belfast Festival at Queen's) and in the period 1965–67 Festival Publications issued a first series of poetry pamphlets by Seamus Heaney, Michael Longley, Derek Mahon, James Simmons, Philip Hobsbaum, Arthur Terry, Stewart Parker, Joan Newmann and Seamus Deane. A second series followed, to which the contributors included Laurence Lerner, Norman Buller,

Arthur Terry and Norman Dugdale, but also Irish poets like John Montague and John Hewitt who were not directly associated with the Group; a third featured further pamphlets by James Simmons and Stewart Parker, but also work by the leading Scottish poets George Mackay Brown and Ian Crichton-Smith. Indeed the Belfast Festival at Queen's, supported by the Arts Council of Northern Ireland, has continued, over forty years, to play a vital role in the development of poetry at the University, most notably through its programme of readings and lectures.

The impact of Festival Publications, which gave profile and visibility to a generation of talented poets, serves as a reminder that poetry cannot flourish without printed outlets. The story of poetry at Queen's is, in part, the story of the small magazines, some durable, some short-lived, which were often the initial platform for emerging poets. The first significant literary magazine based at the University was *The Northman*, founded in 1926 and issuing its final number in 1950. Roy McFadden refers in interview to his 'group of peers gathered around *The Northman* at Queen's', Robert Greacen and John Gallen edited the magazine for a time and John Hewitt's poetry and prose appeared there regularly in the 1930s and 1940s. Many of the local writers who published in *The Northman* were later, as graduates, associated with influential Belfast-based magazines such as *Lagan* (1945–46), of which Hewitt was poetry editor, and *Rann* (1948–53), which was founded and co-edited by McFadden.

The vacuum created by the demise of *The Northman* was filled mainly by the magazines *Q*, founded in 1950 by H.A. Barrington and Victor Price, *Interest* and *Gorgon*. Early work by Heaney, Deane and Parker appeared in such magazines in the late 1950s and early 1960s, some of Heaney's pieces bearing the pseudonym 'Incertus'. *The Northern Review* (1965–67), which was founded and edited by Ian Hill and Mike Mitchell, ran to three issues and featured work by members of Hobsbaum's Group, and in 1967 Harry Chambers, a lecturer in English at Stranmillis College and a former member of the Group, revived his magazine *Phoenix*, devoting the first issue to the arts in Ulster. Shortly afterwards Chambers returned to England but continued, until the magazine ceased publication in 1995, to publish Group members, including pamphlet collections by Heaney and Longley. An issue of the Lyric Theatre magazine *Threshold*, published in 1969 and guest-edited by Heaney, further reflected the energies and continuities of the period: Heaney reviewed Hewitt's *Collected Poems 1932–67*, the Group writers were strongly represented and the issue contained some of Paul Muldoon's earliest published poems.

Muldoon's first poems in print had already appeared in *The Honest Ulsterman*, founded by James Simmons in 1968; at the end of 1969, the editorship of the magazine passed to Michael Foley and the present writer, both of whom had had their first poems published there and both of whom were undergraduate, then postgraduate students of Queen's in their first few years as editors. The magazine went on to survive the century, during which time it published most of the Ulster poets who had sprung to prominence in the 1940s, 1950s and 1960s, and it became the main local outlet for those who emerged in the 1970s and 1980s, including Muldoon, Ciaran Carson and Medbh McGuckian, as well as new Ulster poets not associated with Queen's such as Tom Paulin, William Peskett and Robert Johnstone. The Ulsterman Publications imprint took up where Festival Publications left off, issuing numerous pamphlet collections, mainly by Northern Irish, but also by Irish, English and Scottish poets and poets of other nationalities over a period of some thirty-five years. The independent review *Fortnight*, which was founded in 1970 by Tom Hadden, a lecturer in law at Queen's University Belfast, and which is still in existence, proved another valuable outlet for poetry and carried reviews of collections by Ulster poets; its literary editors have included James Simmons, Medbh McGuckian and Moyra Donaldson.

The presence of the American novelist William Wiser as writer in residence at the University from 1979 to 1982 coincided with and nurtured the emergence of yet another generation of undergraduate writers, including the poets John Hughes, Andrew Elliott and Damian Smyth, and others such as Damian Gorman and Kevin Smith who have not yet published book-length collections. The student magazine *Outlines*, three issues of which appeared between 1980 and 1982, provided an early platform for this group. *Outlines* begat *Tangier*, edited by John Hughes, which begat *North*, also edited by Hughes. In 1982 Damian Gorman produced the first issue of *The Belfast Review*, which until 1986 included a poetry supplement edited by Patrick Williams. The student newspaper *Gown*, which had published poetry sporadically since the 1950s, produced the *Gown Literary Supplement* in the 1980s and early 1990s, out of which emerged *The Big Spoon* in 1993. Martin Mooney, who was a co-editor of both publications, also co-founded the poetry magazine *Rhinoceros* in 1988. In 2005 the Seamus Heaney Centre for Poetry issued the first volume of its annual literary journal *The Yellow Nib*, under the general editorship of Ciaran Carson.

Where writers gather, magazines and broadsheets proliferate and the foregoing survey of such publishing activity at or on the periphery of Queen's is by no means comprehensive. I think, for example, of *Snakes Alive*, a Medical Faculty magazine which published creative work, of *Crab Grass*, a quirky, inventive publication produced by John Gilbert, Marcus Patton and others in the late 1960s and early 1970s, of the broadsheet *Fusion*, two issues of which appeared in the late 1960s, of *Graticule*, a Department of Geography magazine which included literary material and of Carol Rumens's magazine *Brangle*. The work begun by such publications is often consolidated in anthologies and books and a notable development in recent years has been the appearance of compendia such as *The Hauling Songs* (2000), published by the English Society at Queen's and presenting poetry and prose by members of the Queen's Writers' Group while Daragh Carville was writer in residence. Carville has also edited *New Soundings: An Anthology of New Writing from the North of Ireland*, published by Blackstaff Press in 2003.

It should, perhaps, be recorded here that several of the most prominent local presses engaged in poetry publishing since the early 1970s have strong connections with Queen's. Anne Tannahill, who was managing director of Blackstaff Press from 1980 to 2003, is a graduate and postgraduate of Queen's and the current managing editor Patricia Horton took her doctorate in the School of English there. Lagan Press was founded in 1990 by Pat Ramsey, who graduated in 1986, and Summer Palace Press, which is located in County Donegal, was started by Joan and Kate Newmann, both of whom are represented in this anthology.

A number of gifted teachers have significantly influenced the course of poetry at Queen's. Helen Waddell blossomed under the encouragement of Gregory Smith, Professor of English during her time as an undergraduate. Philip Hobsbaum's role in the 1960s has already been noted. Seamus Heaney has paid tribute to Professor John Braidwood, who inspired in him a lasting interest in Old English and Anglo-Saxon poetry, and also Matthew McDiarmid under whom he studied Wordsworth. Both Heaney and Seamus Deane were also stimulated by the South African poet Laurence Lerner, who taught at Queen's from 1953 to 1962, partly because his lectures reflected his experience of a divided society in ways that had local resonance. Later generations of Queen's-educated poets have benefited from the presence in the English Department of Michael Allen and Edna Longley, who provided not only a strong critical grounding in English, Irish and American poetry but also the kind of individual attention and practical advice that is invaluable to emerging talent. The active nurturing of new voices has been particularly evident since the 1970s in the appointment, jointly with the Arts Council of Northern Ireland, of poets, novelists and dramatists as writers in residence in both the English Department and the Department of Celtic and Irish Studies, and the University now provides an MA course in Creative Writing.

Several of the writers in residence (William Wiser, Carol Rumens, Colin Teevan) have come from outside the north of Ireland and any survey of poetry at Queen's must register this healthy receptivity to the wider community of poets. It is reflected also in, for example, the work of translators such as Helen Waddell, Arthur Terry and G. Singh, in the pages of many of the publications mentioned earlier and in the way writers' groups at the University have welcomed talent from outside the student and academic body. Since the early 1970s, an adventurous English Society has worked in conjunction with the Arts Council of Northern Ireland to attract a dazzling variety of writers and lecturers to the University, and the poets John Montague, Nuala Ní Dhómhnaill and Paul Durcan have each spent a semester on campus as Ireland Professor of Poetry. As noted earlier, the status of poetry at the University was given an additional boost by the founding of the Seamus Heaney Centre for Poetry in 2003, with Ciaran Carson as its first Director.

*

The purpose of this anthology is to reflect the richness and diversity of poetry at Queen's University Belfast since the early twentieth century and in particular the remarkable flowering that had its origins in the 1960s and has continued through every decade since.

The core contributors are poets of international repute, such as Helen Waddell (as translator), John Hewitt, Seamus Heaney, Michael Longley, Paul Muldoon, Ciaran Carson and Medbh McGuckian. The anthology also includes a wide range of poets who have published at least one separate book-length collection in English or Irish. The majority of those represented are former students or graduates of the University but I have, in addition, included the work of poets and translators who served on the staff there, such as Philip Larkin, Laurence Lerner, Philip Hobsbaum, W.J. Harvey, Arthur Terry and G. Singh. A number of other distinguished non-Queen's graduates, such as James Simmons, Carol Rumens, Cathal Ó Searcaigh and Sinead Morrissey, have been employed by Queen's as writers in residence and their inclusion is intended as an acknowledgement of their immensely significant contribution to poetry in the University.

Among the poets already included as graduates, Helen Waddell, John Hewitt, Seamus Heaney and Paul Muldoon have been awarded honorary degrees by the University. Four other poets have been accorded this honour: W.B. Yeats, Lascelles Abercrombie, Louis MacNeice and Michael Longley. Of those I have included only Michael Longley, who, as a member of the Belfast Group, active participant in the English Society over four decades and Literature Officer for the Arts Council of Northern Ireland, has been central to the development of poetry at Queen's.

The anthology has been compiled as a sampler or showcase and does not pretend to rank poets canonically in terms of critical reputation. Neither is the selection of poets exhaustive, in that many other poet-graduates have published in pamphlet form or been included in introductory anthologies such as the *Trio* series published by Blackstaff Press.

I gratefully acknowledge the practical and critical support of Ciaran Carson and the Seamus Heaney Centre for Poetry, Peter Cavan, Tom Collins, Director of Marketing, Recruitment and Communications at Queen's and his staff, Sir Peter Froggatt, Ian Hill, Edna Longley, Michael Longley, Robert Greacen, Victor Price, Pat Ramsey and Anne Tannahill.

FRANK ORMSBY

# HELEN WADDELL
## 1889–1965

### EPITAPH FOR HIS NIECE, SOPHIA

Dewy the earth with tears
  That holds thee, precious one.
The jewel of our years,
  All grace with thee is gone.
From thy first spring so lovely and so wise
  The old men stayed to hear thy soft replies.
What other maids scarce learn by length of days,
  Was thine without delays.
So dying, thou hast been thy grandam's death,
  Thee dead, she would not draw reluctant breath.
    Love had the marriage bed
    Already for thee spread,
And I had hoped to live to see thy son.
  Alas, O little maid, for marriage bed
We gave to thee a grave,
  For wedding torch, lit candles at thy head,
    For laughter, wringing hands,
      Tears for the singing lyre,
        For music, moan.
The cruel frost hath killed our budding vine
  And the wild winds have strewn our crimson rose.

*from the Latin of Paul the Deacon (c. 720–800)*

1

## LAMENT FOR HATHIMODA, ABBESS OF GANDESHEIM

Thou hast come safe to port,
    I still at sea.
The light is on thy head,
    Darkness in me.
Pluck thou in heaven's field
    Violet and rose
While I strew flowers that will thy vigil keep
    Where thou dost sleep
    Love in thy last repose.

*from the Latin: Anonymous (ninth century)*

2

# JOHN HEWITT

## 1907–1987

### SUBSTANCE AND SHADOW

There is a bareness in the images
I temper time with in my mind's defence;
they hold their own, their stubborn secrecies;
no use to rage against their reticence:
a gannet's plunge, a heron by a pond,
a last rook homing as the sun goes down,
a spider squatting on a bracken-frond,
and thistles in a cornsheaf's tufted crown,
a boulder on a hillside, lichen-stained,
the sparks of sun on dripping icicles,
their durable significance contained
in texture, colour, shape, and nothing else.
All these are sharp, spare, simple, native to
this small republic I have charted out
as the sure acre where my sense is true,
while round its boundaries sprawl the screes
   of doubt.

My lamp lights up the kettle on the stove
and throws its shadow on the whitewashed wall,
like some Assyrian profile with, above,
a snake, or bird-prowed helmet crested tall;
but this remains a shadow; when I shift
the lamp or move the kettle it is gone,
the substance and the shadow break adrift
that needed bronze to lock them, bronze or stone.

3

# THE KING'S HORSES

After fifty years, nearly, I remember,
living then in a quiet leafy suburb,
waking in the darkness, made aware
of a continuous irregular noise,
and groping to the side window to discover
the shadow-shapes which made that muffled patter
passing across the end of our avenue,
the black trees and the streetlights shuttering
a straggle of flowing shadows, endless, of horses.

Gypsies they could have been, or tinkers maybe,
mustering to some hosting of their clans,
or horse-dealers heading their charges to the docks,
timed to miss the day's traffic and alarms;
a migration the newspapers had not foretold;

some battle's ragged finish, dream repeated;
the last of an age retreating, withdrawing,
leaving us beggared, bereft
of the proud nodding muzzles, the nervous bodies;
gone from us the dark men with their ancient skills
of saddle and stirrup, of bridle and breeding.

It was an end, I was sure, but an end of what
I never could tell. It was never reported;
but the echoing hooves persisted. Years after,
in a London hotel in the grey dawn
a serious man concerned with certain duties,
I heard again the metal clatter of hooves staccato

4

and hurriedly rose to catch a glimpse of my horses,
but the pace and beat were utterly different:
I saw by the men astride these were the King's horses
going about the King's business, never mine.

# W.R. RODGERS

## 1909–1969

*from* RESURRECTION:
AN EASTER SEQUENCE

*And there was Mary Magdalene and the other Mary, sitting over
against the sepulchre . . .*

It is always the women who are the Watchers
And Keepers of life, they guard our exits
And our entrances. They are both tomb and womb,
End and beginning. Bitterly they bring forth
And bitterly take back the light they gave.
The last to leave and still the first to come.
They circle us like sleep or like the grave.
Earth is their element, and in it lies
The seed and silence of the lighted skies,
The seasons with their fall and slow uprise,
Man with his sight and militant surmise.
It is always the women who are the Watchers
And Wakeners . . .

# FIELD DAY

The old farmer, nearing death, asked
To be carried outside and set down
Where he could see a certain field
'And then I will cry my heart out,' he said.

It troubles me, thinking about that man;
What shape was the field of his crying
In Donegal?

I remember a small field in Down, a field
Within fields, shaped like a triangle.
I could have stood there and looked at it
All day long.

And I remember crossing the frontier between
France and Spain at a forbidden point, and seeing
A small triangular field in Spain,
And stopping

Or walking in Ireland down any rutted by-road
To where it hit the highway, there was always

At this turning-point and abutment
A still centre, a V-shape of grass
Untouched by cornering traffic,
Where country lads larked at night.

I think I know what the shape of the field was
That made the old man weep.

# ROBERT GREACEN

## b.1920

### ST ANDREW'S DAY

St Andrew's Day, blind November fumbling
The hurt leaves, bleached gutter orphans.
Half-light domesticates raw brick.
A mediocre day, not to be remembered.
It's 2 p.m. at Ladbroke Grove. I board a bus.
The mourners are gathering at Glengarriff.
Is it drizzling there? I hear the rain
Touch-typing an elegy on the Bay waters.
Though in her will she said 'no flowers'
Our daughter will place veronica on the coffin
Borne through the woods to the Old Killeen.
Will the funeral go to plan, discreetly,
Even in the drizzle I imagine falling
On the lands of Gael and Planter?
I say a London goodbye to a lost wife,
Remember our time of roses, promises,
The silvered sea at Ardnagashel,
Earrings of fuchsia in the hedgerows,
Hope arching like a rainbow over all.

## CARNIVAL AT THE RIVER

The procession of ghosts shuffles by,
Faceless, bannerless, blobs in a landscape
Of dead trees, rotted flowers.
Gradually the blobs dissolve into people.
Father steps out in Edwardian style,
Links arms with Mother in her flowered hat.
There's cousin Jim, his gun lusting for snipe.
Aunt Tillie's fox fur dangles at her neck.
Teachers pace by in funereal gowns,
Boys in uniform, bare-kneed, sulk past
As if they'd been cheated of a holiday.
Stewart pushes a 1930s Raleigh bike,
Willie McIlwaine drools over an oval ball.
I turn on my side and hope for easy sleep
Away from the images of childhood
But the procession sidles into dream.
I am walking beside Grandfather.
He plucks his goatee, tells me softly:
'We're going to the carnival.
We are gathering at the river.'
I feel cold, my guts tighten.
Father's father, take my arm!
Grandfather holds me, quotes Beckett:
'*Je n'ai rien contre les cimetières*'.
We laugh, walk arm in arm to the carnival,
The gathering at the river.

9

# ROY McFADDEN
## 1921–1999


### MY MOTHER'S YOUNG SISTER

*A new decade,* the teacher cried,
Clapping chalk from her hands.
Then: *1930.* Someone laughed
Uncertainly; the rest of us were awed.

By 1939 we'd be
Coping with Life, she said.
Did I hold back a thought for you
Trapped in the Twenties, young Persephone?

My youth, not yours, is stirred again
By summer photographs,
Items of Twentyish furniture,
That outfaced decades you have never known.

But, in sleep's undertone, you came,
Sidestepping memory,
Vivid, vivacious; unperturbed
By futures come and gone after your time.

And I caught at your perfume, and
Half-heard the teacher say
*You are a shade too old for him:*
Above my head, as though *you'd* understand.

But such discrepancy in years
Death stands upon its head:
You, twenty-three for ever now,
My age careering towards my grandfather's.

You were a girl who hurried past
My childhood, with a dream's
Inconstancy; as if forewarned,
Time being short, you had to travel fast.

# THE HUNGER-MARCHERS

Throughout the house, residual books
Left from my father's library
Memorialise those early years
When life, believably perfectible,
Beckoned with promises,
And courteous futures held out welcoming doors.

Dated in his punctilious hand
*1911*, *'12*, they've earned
Shelf-room not just as literature –
Small, florin classics, once so proudly bought,
Brought home as honoured guests –
But also for his resolute signature.

Sheet-music of my mother's, notes
From singing lessons, recipes
For moral and material good,
Minutes of meetings in decrepit halls,
The lonely public voice:
Their presence is a quickening of the blood –

As when the small boy piper led
The hunger-marchers from the north,
Dancing ahead on bandaged feet;
And hope lined kerbstones, craned from windowsills,
Clapped liberated hands,
And children's cheers like flowers decked the street.

# PHILIP LARKIN
## 1922–1985

## CHURCH GOING

Once I am sure there's nothing going on
I step inside, letting the door thud shut.
Another church: matting, seats, and stone,
And little books; sprawlings of flowers, cut
For Sunday, brownish now; some brass and stuff
Up at the holy end; the small neat organ;
And a tense, musty, unignorable silence,
Brewed God knows how long. Hatless, I take off
My cycle-clips in awkward reverence,

Move forward, run my hand around the font.
From where I stand, the roof looks almost new –
Cleaned, or restored? Someone would know: I don't.
Mounting the lectern, I peruse a few
Hectoring large-scale verses, and pronounce
'Here endeth' much more loudly than I'd meant.
The echoes snigger briefly. Back at the door
I sign the book, donate an Irish sixpence,
Reflect the place was not worth stopping for.

Yet stop I did: in fact I often do,
And always end much at a loss like this,
Wondering what to look for; wondering, too,
When churches fall completely out of use

What we shall turn them into, if we shall keep
A few cathedrals chronically on show,
Their parchment, plate and pyx in locked cases,
And let the rest rent-free to rain and sheep.
Shall we avoid them as unlucky places?

Or, after dark, will dubious women come
To make their children touch a particular stone;
Pick simples for a cancer; or on some
Advised night see walking a dead one?
Power of some sort or other will go on
In games, in riddles, seemingly at random;
But superstition, like belief, must die,
And what remains when disbelief has gone?
Grass, weedy pavement, brambles, buttress, sky,

A shape less recognisable each week,
A purpose more obscure. I wonder who
Will be the last, the very last, to seek
This place for what it was; one of the crew
That tap and jot and know what rood-lofts were?
Some ruin-bibber, randy for antique,
Or Christmas-addict, counting on a whiff
Of gowns-and-bands and organ-pipes and myrrh?
Or will he be my representative,

Bored, uninformed, knowing the ghostly silt
Dispersed, yet tending to this cross of ground
Through suburb scrub because it held unspilt
So long and equably what since is found
Only in separation – marriage, and birth,

14

And death, and thoughts of these – for which was built
This special shell? For, though I've no idea
What this accoutred frowsty barn is worth,
It pleases me to stand in silence here;

A serious house on serious earth it is,
In whose blent air all our compulsions meet,
Are recognised, and robed as destinies.
And that much never can be obsolete,
Since someone will forever be surprising
A hunger in himself to be more serious,
And gravitating with it to this ground,
Which, he once heard, was proper to grow wise in,
If only that so many dead lie round.

## REASONS FOR ATTENDANCE

The trumpet's voice, loud and authoritative,
Draws me a moment to the lighted glass
To watch the dancers – all under twenty-five –
Shifting intently, face to flushed face,
Solemnly on the beat of happiness.

– Or so I fancy, sensing the smoke and sweat,
The wonderful feel of girls. Why be out here?
But then, why be in there? Sex, yes, but what
Is sex? Surely, to think the lion's share
Of happiness is found by couples – sheer

Inaccuracy, as far as I'm concerned.
What calls me is that lifted, rough-tongued bell
(Art, if you like) whose individual sound
Insists I too am individual.
It speaks; I hear; others may hear as well,

But not for me, nor I for them; and so
With happiness. Therefore I stay outside,
Believing this; and they maul to and fro,
Believing that; and both are satisfied,
If no one has misjudged himself. Or lied.

# W.J. HARVEY
## 1925–1967


### ARRIVING AT LARNE: SEASICK

The land befouls its frontier; from the deck
I watch marauding gulls contend for swill;
a scum of oil recurdles in our swell,
the cranes like cripples bend above the dock.

Christ, what a country! Gross beyond the quay
gasometers like bulging tumours blotch
the tiers of gaudy houses – all a botched-
up, slap-dash canvas of decay.

But never godforsaken; through gauze rain
probe hypodermic spires – not quite condemned
this limbo landscape, possibly redeemed
where from the mountain's black and basalt groin
aseptic snow may purge polluted soil,
and rivers vent to sea their human bile.

# LAURENCE LERNER

## b.1925

### RASPBERRIES

Once, as a child, I ate raspberries. And forgot.
And then, years later,
A raspberry flowered on my palate, and the past
Burst in unfolding layers within me.
It tasted of grass and honey.
You were there, watching and smiling.
Our love unfolded in the taste of raspberries.

More years have passed; and you are far, and ill;
And I, unable to reach you, eating raspberries.
Their dark damp red, their cool and fragile fur
On the always edge of decay, on the edge of bitter,
Bring a hush of taste to the mouth

Tasting of earth and of crushed leaves
Tasting of summer's insecurity,
Tasting of crimson, dark with the smell of honey

Tasting of childhood and of remembered childhood,
And now, now first, the darker taste of dread.

Sap and imprisoned sunlight and crushed grass
Lie on my tongue like a shadow,
Burst like impending news on my aching palate

18

Tasting not only of death (I could bear that)
But of death and of you together,
The folded layers of love and the sudden future,
Tasting of earth and the thought of you as earth

As I go on eating, waiting for the news.

# IN MEMORIAM: 17 JUNE 1977

Von Braun is dead; the elders are in flower.

A ball of fire exploding in the night
Left its soft trail. Below, a house disgorged
Plaster and teeth, pots, lino, chair-legs, dust,
And bones and blood into the dark.
A jar of elder wine was vaporised.
It was my uncle's house in SE10.
Above, sparks tumbled, fading in the noise.

The troops moved in, and sulked; and everywhere
The women sulked in German.
The men they'd killed for killing them were gone.
Did they expect a welcome? Only the white
Tumultuous blossom on the elder spoke.
Von Braun surrendered to a private; took
His tanks of fuel, his notebooks, and his team
Of tumbling rockets, clicked his heels, and said
'I am Von Braun. Take me to Mister Truman'.

He tossed his rockets up: some on the moon
And some on London. Some are singeing space,
Some stream around us, some came tumbling down,
One on my uncle.  Out of his box of bones
He fell in shreds.
He drank his elder wine through every pore.

Uncle, here is a message. June has come,
Your sons are well, two men are on the moon,
There is a car park where your house once stood,
Von Braun is dead, the elders are in flower.

# G. SINGH

## b.1926

### THE CARILLON PENDULUM CLOCK

The old pendulum clock with the carillon
came from France perhaps
at the time of the Second Empire.
So faint was its voice that it neither
trilled nor pealed but exhaled
instead of sounding, the entrance
of Escamillo or the bells of Corneville
which were its novelty when someone bought it,
perhaps the great-grandfather who ended up
in a lunatic asylum and was buried
without regrets, obituary or other
such notices which might have embarrassed
his unborn grandchildren. They came later
and lived without remembering him
who carried that object within
inhospitable walls lashed by
the furies of the southwest gales
– and which of them heard its alarm?

It was a call that of course woke no one who wasn't
Already awake. Only I, being always sleepless,
heard one dawn the vocal ectoplasm,
the echo of the *toriada*, but just for a second.
Then the voice from the case didn't die out

but spoke almost inaudibly and said
there isn't a spring nor electric charge
that won't run down one day.
I who was Time, abandon it,
and say to you, my only listener,
try to live outside of time,
which no one can measure. Then the voice
was silent and the clock remained
hung on the wall for years.
Probably one can still trace its outline
    on the plaster.

      *from the Italian of Eugenio Montale (1896–1981)*

## IN THE SMOKE

How often I waited for you
at the station in the cold and fog,
strolled up and down, coughing, buying papers
not even worth the name,
smoking Giuba, later banned by the minister
of tobacco, what a fool!
Perhaps a wrong train, or an extra section,
or one that was simply cancelled.
I'd peer at the trolleys of the porters
to see if your luggage was there,
and you, coming late, behind it.
And there you were at last!
One memory this among many.
It pursues me in my dreams.

*from the Italian of Eugenio Montale (1896–1981)*

## ARTHUR TERRY

### 1927–2004

### A SMALL WAR

They were carrying anti-tank mines,
heavy and useless, like historic symbols,
covered in blankets thick with the timeless smell
of herbs and mule sweat. Also machine guns
and Stens made in England.
In twos and threes, at straggling intervals,
minute and diligent as lice on a fallen tree,
the Maquis were crossing the Pyrenees.
It was one of the smallest wars we have ever known.
Only a single body came my way. That of
a country girl from Aragon, who got a lift
in an army truck, and became another
obvious symbol. The driver and mechanic
were careless, and the three of them went through
  a bridge.
The girl had a simple lesion, nothing of interest,
but the doctors who did the post-mortem
found on one ankle a remarkable growth
of hereditary origin, rooted deep in the tree of her race.
And a moment's pain, and the pleasure before it,
seemed small when compared with that defect
  of centuries,
working in silence. Nothing personal, mind.
It was war, though a small one.

And, though it was strange, there was nothing
    personal, either,
in the shock that I felt for a moment during the inquest,
feeling the sun beat down on the shed by the wall,
on the tangled stubble of crosses and bones
in that village cemetery, where the stench of death
smelt like an unwashed crotch.
It just meant I was young, like most who go to wars,
who are scared of the flesh, and destroy and abuse it.
All, in a word, emblematic, eternal.

*from the Catalan of Gabriel Ferrater (1922–72)*

26

# TIME WAS

Let me escape into your old domain.
Our ghosts still drift about the usual place.
I see the winter sky, the metal footbridge
with its blackened struts, the scurf of grass
along the burnt-up track. I hear the express whistle.
Its gathering thunder rocks the ground we stand on
till we have to shout. We watch it pass.
Your soundless laughter sets me laughing too.
I see your dove-grey blouse, the blue
of your short flared skirt, the red scarf bunched
around your neck, the one I used to call
your country's flag.
All's as it was that day. The words we said
come back, and now, the one bad moment.
Something has silenced us. You've hurt your hand.
Remember how it fluttered and hung limp,
nervously fingering your cycle bell.
It's just as well we're interrupted.
Now, as before, the tramp of metal heels,
the outsize chant of men in battle dress,
steel-helmeted, surrounds us. A command
darts out like the savage glitter of a snake,
and we hide our faces in the lap of fear
till they have passed. Now we've forgotten
how we were: their unreflecting movement
restores us to ourselves, and we are glad
to be together in this place, not caring if we speak.

So we may kiss. We're young: those distant silences
have no authority;
the fear of others kills our private fears.
Freewheeling down the avenue, we feel the cold
as each tree spreads its heavy mass of shade.
We glide from chill to chill, unconsciously.

*from the Catalan of Gabriel Ferrater (1922–72)*

# VICTOR PRICE
## b.1930

### JEANIE

Reared on the gospel and small-town decorum,
She viewed the universe with grave alarm,
Holding her prayer-book like a talisman
Aslant her bodice in a white-gloved hand.
But she could not escape. My grandfather,
A thin-legged schoolmaster with mad flecks
In the pupils of his pale blue eyes,
Frightened her one day into marriage.
She suffered the indignity of sex.

Forty years and three daughters later,
When the tight-wound spring in his head
Had sent him reeling into suicide,
She fetched up in a golden age, coming
To live with her second child, my mother.
The stateliness of her middle years dissolved;
Age shrank her, rounding her shoulders
For blows that never came, but seeming
To draw all her goodness to a point:
She was a russet apple full of juice
With hale cheeks only a little wrinkled.

A sly ingenuous humour, submerged
In troubled times, broke surface now;

The quaint sayings of a distant past –
Her green ones, we called them – became
Her stock in trade. She moved about the house
With the loving hilarity of an old nun.

And then senility. She died in hospital
Incontinent – her only indiscretion;
Not knowing us – her only selfishness.

# JAMES ELLIS

## b.1931

### OVER THE BRIDGE
*for Paddy Devlin*

I crossed a bridge and thought to shake the dust
From off my feet, but it was not to be;
For though I fled across the Irish Sea,
Nursing resentment and profound disgust

That individuals had betrayed their trust
And held the public stage in ignominy,
Events o'ertook the ancient enemy,
And time has mellowed memory, as it must.

Homeward I crawl, a wretched prodigal,
To bide awhile, and then again depart –
To leave once more, once more to feel bereft –

Your picture album in my mental holdall,
The hills of Antrim etched upon my heart,
For truth to tell, I never really left.

# JAMES FENTON
## b.1931


### WATTER QUAIL

A fissle unther the deed, saft-hingin thatch,
A strippit shedda, a wheekin scad,
Ye jook crootched an shairp an quait
Amang the queelrods.

Or, ower late, ower scarred, tae
Rin, ye flitter up,
A soonless flachter,
A thaveless, loast flaffin nixt
Naewhur, lang legs hingin silly, or aiblins glammin
The empy air for
A graip o the sure wat grun, tae
Ye drap, or fa, bak
Inty the cowl shilter o the deed
Staks, fleein frae sicht, yit naw
The licht itsel.

For, wae the dark creepin, quait
As daith,
Frae oot the boag, amang the queelrods an
A' ower yer wuthered worl,
Comes thon ra, rivin screch –
Agane the nicht's comin? Or

Whut the nicht micht bring? Or
Wull bring?

Whutiver:
The yin cry'll dae
Iz baith, wer lane
In the getherin dark.

# PHILIP HOBSBAUM
## 1932–2005


## THE ASTIGMATIC

At seven the sun that lit my world blew out
Leaving me only mist. Through which I probed
My way to school, guessed wildly at the sums
Whose marks on the board I couldn't even see.

They wanted to send me away to a special school.
I refused, and coped as best I could with half
The light lost in the mist, screwing my tears
Into my work, my gritted teeth, my writing –

Which crawled along and writhed. Think
   thoughts at will,
None of it comes across. Even now friends ask
'How do you read that scrawl?' The fact is, I don't;
Nobody could. I guess. But how would you

Like my world where parallels actually join,
Perspectives vary at sight? Once in a pub
I walked towards a sign marked gents over
A grating and crashed through the floor –

Well, it looked all right to me. Those steep stairs
People told me of later flattened to lines
In my half-world. The rest imagination
Supplied: when you've half a line you extend it.

The lenses drag their framework down my nose.
I still can't look strangers in the face,
Wilting behind a wall of glass at them.
It makes me look shifty at interviews.

I wake up with a headache, chew all day
Aspirins, go to bed dispirited,
Still with a dull pain somewhere in my skull,
And sleep. Then, in my dreams, the sun comes out.

# GIRL REPORTER

Fact is her fiction. Sitting in the bar
Raincoat still on, crossed nylon legs revealing
Less than we think, a male in tow and smiling –
Her narrowed eyes flick past to register
Whether I am a story in the offing.

Life is material for her creation.
The doll by the upturned scooter – that is real,
Its head, see, stains the kerb. She runs to call
The news-desk first, then after the police-station,
Already mapping the story of the trial.

Errors of fact are part of her prose style.
With every slashing cross-head some truth dies.
In love? She knows. You hate her? She knows. You'll
Cure cancer? Reach the moon? Her face may smile –
You're placed by those all-knowing know-all eyes.

What chance has truth against such showy error?
We're butterflies pinned down by this young lady,
Facts of our lives are melted down for cliché.
Even as I write her gaze observes my tremor –
Her lethal pencil always at the ready.

# JAMES SIMMONS
## 1933–2001


### DIDN'T HE RAMBLE

*for Michael Longley*

'The family wanted to make a bricklayer of him, but Ferd. was
too smooth and clever a fellow. He preferred to sit in the parlour
out of the sun and play piano.'

HENRY MORTON

There was a hardware shop in Main Street sold
records as well as spades and plastic bowls.
Jo, the assistant, had a taste for jazz.

The shop being empty as it mostly was
I tried out records, then, like seeing the light,
but genuine, I heard Josh White:
I'M GOING TO MO-O-VE YOU, WAY ON THE
    OUTSKIRTS OF TOWN.
Where was my turntable to set it down!
A voice styled by experience, learning to make
music listening to Blind Willie Blake,
walking the streets of a city, avoiding cops,
toting a cheap guitar and begging box.

The campus poets used to write of saxophones
disgustedly and sneer at gramophones;
but the word of life, if such a thing existed,

was there on record among the rubbish listed
in the catalogues of Brunswick and HMV,
healing the split in sensibility.
Tough reasonableness and lyric grace
together, in poor man's dialect.
Something that no one taught us to expect.
Profundity without the po-face
of court and bourgeois modes. This I could use
to live and die with. Jazz. Blues.
I love the music and the men who made
the music, and instruments they played:
saxophone, piano, trumpet, clarinet,
Bill Broonzy, Armstrong, Basie, Hodges, Chet
Baker, Garner, Tommy Ladnier,
Jelly Roll Morton, Bessie Smith, Bechet,
and Fats Waller, the scholar-clown of song
who sang 'Until the Real Thing Comes Along'.
Here was the risen people, their feet
dancing, not out to murder the elite:
'Pardon me, sir, may we be free?
The kitchen staff is having a jamboree'.

History records how people cleared the shelves
of record shops, discovering themselves,
making distinctions in the ordinary,
seeing what they'd been too tired to see;
but most ignored the music. Some were scared,
some greedy, some condemned what they hadn't
    heard,
some sold cheap imitations, watered it down,
bribed Fats to drink too much and play the clown

instead of the piano, and failed – the man was wise,
he did both painlessly. Jazz is a compromise:
you take the first tune in your head and play
until it's saying what you want to say.
'I ain't got no diplomas,' said Satchmo,
'I look into my heart and blow.'

What if some great ones took to drugs and drink
and killed themselves? Only a boy could think
the world cures easy, and want to blame
someone. I know I'll never be the same.
A mad world, my masters! We might have known
that Wardell Gray was only well spoken,
controlled and elegant on saxophone.
He appeared last in a field with his neck broken.
The jazz life did it, not the Ku Klux Klan.
Whatever made the music killed the man.

## STEPHANO REMEMBERS

We broke out of our dream into a clearing
and there were all our masters still sneering.
My head bowed, I made jokes and turned away,
living over and over that strange day.

The ship struck before morning. Half past four,
on a huge hogshead of claret I swept ashore
like an evangelist aboard his god:
his will was mine, I laughed and kissed the rod,
and would have walked that foreign countryside
blind drunk, contentedly till my god died;
but finding Trinculo made it a holiday:
two Neapolitans had got away,
and that shipload of scheming toffs we hated
was drowned. Never to be humiliated
again, 'I will no more to sea,' I sang.
Down white empty beaches my voice rang,
and that dear monster, half fish and half man,
went on his knees to me. Oh, Caliban,
you thought I'd take your twisted master's life;
but a drunk butler's slower with a knife
than your fine courtiers, your dukes, your kings.
We were distracted by too many things …
the wine, the jokes, the music, fancy gowns.
We were no good as murderers, we were clowns.

# JOHN CAMPBELL

## b.1936

### AN OUL JOBBIN' POET

I'm an oul jobbin' poet, born outa my time,
if you buy me a likker, I'll read you a rhyme.
I'm not hard to pay, a wee lager and lime …
If yer flyin', I'll take a quick half-in.

I can render a poem that's fairly well known
or maybe yid like to hear one of me own,
but my throat's kinda raspy and dry as a stone …
just another wee sip … Now we're laughin' …

I know millions of poems, wud you like a wee song?
I've a fine pair of lungs an' a voice that's quite strong.
Just top up me tumbler. It won't take me long.
Pour away. Man, yer hand's fine and steady.

Here's one of me own. It's well written and slick.
An ode guaranteed to bring tears from a brick.
It's all about wimmen who two-time and trick.
Just another wee sip. Then I'm ready.

There's nothin' like wimmen to make a man cringe,
They girn an' they yap if you go on a binge.
When yer sleepin' it off, yer oul ribs get a dinge.
Their ignorance wud drive ye to drinkin'.

Wud ye like to hear 'Cargoes', or maybe 'Drake's Drum'?
Somethin' from Kipling wud make this place hum.
Do you think I cud have a wee coke with this rum?
They tell me it stimulates thinkin'.

I'm an oul jobbin' poet in love with me art,
there's acres of literature locked in me heart.
Just give me a nudge when you want me to start ...
In the meantime, shake a leg with that bottle.

# SEAMUS HEANEY
## b.1939


## A SOFA IN THE FORTIES

All of us on the sofa in a line, kneeling
Behind each other, eldest down to youngest,
Elbows going like pistons, for this was a train

And between the jamb-wall and the bedroom door
Our speed and distance were inestimable.
First we shunted, then we whistled, then

Somebody collected the invisible
For tickets and very gravely punched it
As carriage after carriage under us

Moved faster, *chooka-chook*, the sofa legs
Went giddy and the unreachable ones
Far out on the kitchen floor began to wave.


Ghost-train? Death-gondola? The carved, curved ends,
Black leatherette and ornate gauntness of it
Made it seem the sofa had achieved

Flotation. Its castors on tip-toe,
Its braid and fluent backboard gave it airs
Of superannuated pageantry:

When visitors endured it, straight-backed,
When it stood off in its own remoteness,
When the insufficient toys appeared on it

On Christmas mornings, it held out as itself,
Potentially heavenbound, earthbound for sure,
Among things that might add up or let you down.


We entered history and ignorance
Under the wireless shelf. *Yippee-i-ay*,
Sang 'The Riders of the Range'. HERE IS THE NEWS,

Said the absolute speaker. Between him and us
A great gulf was fixed where pronunciation
Reigned tyrannically. The aerial wire

Swept from a treetop down in through a hole
Bored in the windowframe. When it moved in wind,
The sway of language and its furtherings

Swept and swayed in us like nets in water
Or the abstract, lonely curve of distant trains
As we entered history and ignorance.


We occupied our seats with all our might,
Fit for the uncomfortableness.
Constancy was its own reward already.

Out in front, on the big upholstered arm,
Somebody craned to the side, driver or
Fireman, wiping his dry brow with the air

Of one who had run the gauntlet. We were
The last thing on his mind, it seemed; we sensed
A tunnel coming up where we'd pour through

Like unlit carriages through fields at night,
Our only job to sit, eyes straight ahead,
And be transported and make engine noise.

## POSTSCRIPT

And some time make the time to drive out west
Into County Clare, along the Flaggy Shore,
In September or October, when the wind
And the light are working off each other
So that the ocean on one side is wild
With foam and glitter, and inland among stones
The surface of a slate-grey lake is lit
By the earthed lightning of a flock of swans,
Their feathers roughed and ruffling, white on white,
Their fully grown headstrong-looking heads
Tucked or cresting or busy underwater.
Useless to think you'll park and capture it
More thoroughly. You are neither here nor there,
A hurry through which known and strange things pass
As big soft buffetings come at the car sideways
And catch the heart off guard and blow it open.

# MICHAEL LONGLEY
## b.1939

### CEASEFIRE

#### I

Put in mind of his own father and moved to tears
Achilles took him by the hand and pushed the old king
Gently away, but Priam curled up at his feet and
Wept with him until their sadness filled the building.

#### II

Taking Hector's corpse into his own hands Achilles
Made sure it was washed and, for the old king's sake,
Laid out in uniform, ready for Priam to carry
Wrapped like a present home to Troy at daybreak.

#### III

When they had eaten together, it pleased them both
To stare at each other's beauty as lovers might,
Achilles built like a god, Priam good-looking still
And full of conversation, who earlier had sighed:

#### IV

'I get down on my knees and do what must be done
And kiss Achilles' hand, the killer of my son.'

# THE LEVERET

*for my grandson, Benjamin*

This is your first night in Carrigskeewaun.
The Owennadornaun is so full of rain
You arrived in Paddy Morrison's tractor,
A bumpy approach in your father's arms
To the cottage where, all of one year ago,
You were conceived, a fire-seed in the hearth.
Did you hear the wind in the fluffy chimney?
Do you hear the wind tonight, and the rain
And a shore bird calling from the mussel reefs?
Tomorrow I'll introduce you to the sea,
Little hoplite. Have you been missing it?
I'll park your chariot by the otters' rock
And carry you over seaweed to the sea.
There's a tufted duck on David's lake
With her sootfall of hatchlings, pompoms
A day old and already learning to dive.
We may meet the stoat near the erratic
Boulder, a shrew in his mouth, or the merlin
Meadow-pipit-hunting. But don't be afraid.
The leveret breakfasts under the fuchsia
Every morning, and we shall be watching.
I have picked wild flowers for you, scabious
And centaury in a jam-jar of water
That will bend and magnify the daylight.
This is your first night in Carrigskeewaun.

# GEORGE McWHIRTER
## b.1939

### HOMEWORK

When money was tight, my father hauled
Out the last. Culled ends bought
At Rowan's the shoe-repairers. Ferocious,
Not efficient the new machines bitched up
The leather (infernal fidget of their needles),
He said, and the men hammered the price
Beyond paying. So he carved the soles
Close to his chest, as if scalping an ugly
Enemy skull. Dry slivers
Dropped until the wad was right
For the shoe. Then glue
And nails. My mother melted the ball-black,
Rubbed it over the leather rims, synchronizing
The wax glister with her eyes. On a wooden
Stool she sat, well upholstered by the work
While he smoked, edgy in an armchair. All done
He'd sigh for her being better;
For his spit that spoiled and never polished.

# SEAMUS DEANE
## b.1940

### THE BRETHREN

Arraigned by silence, I recall
The noise of lecture-rooms,
School refectories and dining hall,
A hundred faces in a hundred spoons,
Raised in laughter or in prayer bent,
Each distorted and each innocent.

Torrential sunlight falling through the slats
Made marquetries of light upon the floor.
I still recall those greasy Belfast flats
Where parties hit upon a steady roar
Of subdued violence and lent
Fury to the Sabbath which we spent

Hung over empty streets where Jimmy Witherspoon
Sang under the needle old laments
Of careless love and the indifferent moon,
Evoked the cloudy drumbrush scents
Of Negro brothels while our Plymouth Brethren,
Two doors down, sat sunk in heaven.

Stupor Sunday, *stupor mundi*. What was to come?
The plaints that were growing
Their teeth in the jaws of their aquarium

Sunday's splashless, deep-sown
Peace? What if it were shattered?
Our noise was life and life mattered.

Recently I found old photographs
Fallen behind the attic water-tank
And saw my friends were now the staffs
Of great bureaucracies. Some frames stank
Of mildew, some were so defaced
That half the time I couldn't put a face

On half of them. Some were dead.
The water had seeped through a broken housing,
Had slowly savaged all those eyes and heads.
I felt its rusted coldness dousing
Those black American blues-fired tunes,
The faces echoed in those hammered spoons.

# STEWART PARKER
## 1941–1988

### PADDY DIES

Paddy dies: you never knew him.
A deaf hunchback in a home for the old.

Deafness drew the blind of his soul.
Nobody knew him. Nobody knew him.

A wild animal in him reared
Up one night, I saw his eyes
And for three days he disappeared
They found him sleeping in a pig-sty.
I wonder if sixty years ago
He slept tender in a girl's breasts?

He seems to sleep hard now.
His bony umbrella collapsed at last.

# JOAN NEWMANN
## b.1942

### THE ANGEL OF DEATH

Mary Farquhar burst from the bus
Into our house of sickness.
We had suspended our lives
To let my mother breathe.

Mary Farquhar heard the slow croak,
The thwarted face, erratic heave
Of the patchwork quilt
And spoke of the death rattle.

Mary Farquhar slammed open
Sudden glass on worn sashes.
I escaped to the loanen,
Counting the frayed threads of my blazer:
Watching the open bedroom window
So I might know when to return.

# SABINE WICHERT
## b.1942


## THE SMELL OF FRYING CHEESE

Sometimes she woke to the noise of soldiers
and the alien smell of frying cheese.
They'd bivouac under the ancient trees
by the side of the dirt road. Those oaks
almost saw Napoleon, it was said,
but he didn't quite make it this way. The war
was over, but the locals remained

suspicious. They did not like this freedom –
bringing British soldiers with their gibberish
and gypsies' ways. You could not trust what was
not yours. She, too, had learned to be cautious,
curious, careful, alert and ready
to run as she had had to with her parents

from faraway places bowing to
the patterns of centuries: if you can,
move on. The natives had stayed put, kept their
heads down and survived. By now the soldiers
paid for their eggs, chicken and milk; they had

brought freedom, they said, but no food. Neither
were heroes or rebels watching each other

with beady eyes. By then she had also learnt
to respect but never trust uniforms.

She left before she was quite one of them
and often thought of ancient oaks, the smell
of frying cheese, the need to survive and move on.

# JOHN McGUCKIAN
## b.1943

### IRISH HARE

Just around the time
You might be hoping for a sign,
Unconsciously,
The hare appeared
Very far down in my garden.

Like an omen of goodwill;
Of the hereafter;
That life had a meaning
Beyond;
The hare came up to my window,
And I was startled too.

Death had struck.
She lay like an old doll
On a sofa.
The family gathered around
And I could sense their fear:
Here he comes!

Wasn't I the soft one,
In tears.
And isn't it in my garden
The hare appears.

# CAROL RUMENS
## b.1944


### STEALING THE GENRE

It was the shortest night of the year. I'd been drinking
But I was quite lucid and calm. So, having seen her
The other side of the bar, shedding her light
On no one who specially deserved it, I got to my feet
And simply went over and asked her, in a low voice,
If she'd come to my bed. She raised her eyebrows strangely
But didn't say 'no'. I went out. I felt her follow.

My mind was a storm as we silently crossed the courtyard
In the moist white chill of the dawn. Dear God, I loved her.
I'd loved her in books, I'd adored her at the first sighting.
But no, I'm a woman. English, not young. How could I?
She'd vanished for years. And now she was walking
    beside me.
Oh what am I going to do, what are *we* going to do?
Perhaps she'll know. She's probably an old hand –
But this sudden thought was the most disturbing of all.

As soon as we reached my room, though, it was plain
She hadn't a clue. We stood like window-displays
In our dawn-damp suits with the short, straight,
    hip-hugging skirts
(Our styles are strangely alike, I suppose it's because
Even she has to fight her corner in a man's world)

And discussed the rain, which was coming down, and
    the view,
Which was nothing much, a fuchsia hedge and some trees,
And we watched each other, as women do watch each other,
And tried not to yawn. Why don't you lie down for a bit?
I whispered, inspired. She gratefully kicked off her shoes.

She was onto the bed in no time, and lay as if dumped
On the furthest edge, her face – dear God – to the wall.
I watched for a while, and, thinking she might be in tears,
Caressed the foam-padded viscose that passed for
    her shoulder,
And begged her not to feel guilty. Then I discovered
That all she was doing was breathing, dead to the world.

It wasn't an insult, exactly, but it was a let-down –
And yet I admired her. Sleep. If only I could.
I rested my hand at an uncontroversial location
South of her breasts, maybe north, I don't remember,
And ached with desire and regret and rationalisation.

I'd asked her to bed. And she'd come to bed. End of story.
Only it wasn't the story I'd wanted to tell.
Roll on, tomorrow, I urged, but tomorrow retorted:
I'm here already, and nothing ever gets better.

But then, unexpectedly, I began to feel pleased.
To think she was here, at my side, so condensed, so weighty!
In my humble position (a woman, English, not young,
Et cetera) what more could I ask of an Irish dawn
Than this vision, alive, though dead to the world, on
    my duvet?

What have I done to deserve her? Oh, never mind,
Don't think about words like 'deserve'. So we lay in grace.
The light. Her hair. My hand. Her breath. And the fuchsias.
I thought of the poem I'd write, and fell asleep, smiling.

I woke in a daze of sublime self-congratulation
And saw she was gone. My meadow, my cloud, my aisling!
I could hardly believe my own memory. I wanted to scream
All over the courtyard, come back, come to bed, but how
    could I?
She might be anywhere, people were thick in the day
Already, and things were normal. Why are things normal?

I keened her name to the walls, I swam bitterest rivers,
I buried my face in the cloth where her blushes had slipped
And left a miraculous print that would baffle the laundry:
Oh let me die now. And the dark was all flame as I drank
The heart-breaking odour of Muguets des Bois and
    red wine –
Hers, though I have to admit, it could have been mine.

## PRAYER FOR NORTHERN IRELAND

Night, be starry-sensed for her,
Your bitter frost be fleece to her.
Comb the vale, slow mist, for her.
Lough, be a muscle, tensed for her.

And coals, the only fire in her,
And rain, the only news of her.
Small hills, keep sisters' eyes on her.
Be reticent, desire for her.

Go, stories, leave the breath in her,
The last word to be said by her,
And leave no heart for dead in her.
Steer this ship of dread from her.

No husband lift a hand to her,
No daughter shut the blind on her.
May sails be sewn, seeds grown, for her.
May every kiss be kind to her.

# TOM MATTHEWS
## 1945–2003

### ROBERT SAT

The congregation was scandalised
When Robert sat in his pew and read a paperback

My mother said afterwards
'If he wasn't interested why did he come'

And I marvelled at her
For she never thought of applying that criterion
    to me

And I marvelled at Robert too
Able to read so calmly in the midst of so
    much hate

Robert is now doing very nicely thank you
He emigrated to Canada
And broke both legs in a skiing accident
And married a nurse

# GRÉAGÓIR Ó DÚILL
## b.1946


## SIONNACH

Tráthnóna beag, siúlaimid I dtreo an tábhairne,
Blianta ár gcaidrimh mar chraiceann tiubh ar chomhrá.
Dul ó sholas, agus scáileanna ar thalamh,
Bícearnach codlatach éan, anonn is anall na n-ialtóga.

Chím é, ag siúl na seaniomairí fada, é íseal, ceart,
Trasna ó chlaí go claí, ar a choimhéad ach ag seilg: sionnach.
Imíonn díreach, gan mhoill gan deifre, ar chosa tapa,
Smut íseal, eireaball ag scuabadh drúchta. Stánaimid.

Baineann sé amach an t-ard beag, tiontaíonn,
Amharcann siar orainn faoi amhras, rian den dúshlán ann.
Fios aige nach aon díobháil sinn, téann faoi thom.
Pógaimid. Athraíonn mian. Fillimid at theach.

FOX

At twilight we walk towards the pub.
Our years together add facets to the conversation.
Light fades, shadows lengthen on the fields,
birds bicker, bats bolt by.

We see him, lowslung,
course the lazybeds
from hedge to hedge, hunting on the run,
quick legs at even pace,
nose down, tail brushing dew.
We stare.

From a small height, he turns
to look back at us, unsure, a taste of challenge,
knows we are no threat,
goes out of sight under a whin.

Standing, we kiss, and our desire
sends us back the small road to the house.

*translated from the Irish by Bernie Kenny*

# MICHAEL FOLEY
## b.1947

### THE MIDDLE MANAGER IN PARADISE

Homeostasis finally. System oscillation over. All parameters
at rest.
I have my eternal reward for doing my best

Well earned, with squeezes and cuts and harmonious working
relations to foster
In a time of eroded differentials and deficit-staffing posture

With regular breakdown of normative order, colleagues who
couldn't care less
A total absence of structured complementarity in the
interaction process.

Here it is at last – peace and space with nothing to spoil it
Like running out of tins or having to empty a chemical toilet

And if solitude and empty places give me the blues
There's the first nights, launchings, openings and
anniversary do's.

No need to panic, heaping your plate at the smorgasbord
You can go back as many times as you like and nobody
says a word

Unlimited red/white, sweet/dry sploshing out of your glass
   in the fray
Crushed up against beautiful women who, far from
   turning away

Agree to oral sex when accosted, taking on all comers
And serving them any number of times (single swallows don't
   make summers).

Every taste is catered for.  There's cutprice SM centres
   stocking every line
Braziers, branding-irons, manacles, self-assembly torture racks
   in natural pine.

Though no one's exploited really and of course there's
   no brutality.
Everyone has meaningful relationships and is comfortable
   in their sexuality.

We have consciousness-raising sessions and state-of-the-art
   seminars
Regular small encounter-groups to find and remove
   whatever jars

Recurrent education preventing crises from catching
   us napping
Creating autonomous learners geared to continuous
   environment-shaping.

No one's exempt from our in-service training. Every six weeks
You attend a hands-on workshop in trouble-shooting
   techniques

Simulated stress situations assessed by Barry, the young
    whiz kid:
'I think you were a *shade too directive* there, Ken … *unless of
    course it was a leadership bid'.*

Barry will keep us results-oriented.  Barry won't let us get lax
And take refuge in cognitive dissonance (refusing to face
    facts)

And anyway God's always popping in to see if everything's
    all right
Distinguished and reassuring, goateed, with the voice of an
    acting knight

Showing interest, concern and civility (so much rarer and
    harder than love)
And signing his humorous bestselling autobiography *Heavens
    Above!*

# FRANK ORMSBY
## b.1947


### ONE LOOKS AT ONE

*Gate of Heaven, Valhalla, N.Y.*

She steps from behind a tombstone,
is delicately there,
as though shaped from those sad poems
about dead deer.
I'd like her to stand for the soul,
or forgetful beauty,
or whatever lives without fear,

or simply to stop trembling
and accept the caress
of the way I keep my distance,
muffle the trespass
of even a sudden look.
She watches me sideways,
I ogle a Celtic cross

for as long as it takes to be counted incidental,
then not to count. At last I can watch her pass
unscared into the morning, so tuned to place she
is its sole movement. How soft must be the air
in her fine nostrils. How sweet the cemetery grass.

# CIARAN CARSON

## b.1948

### HAMLET

As usual, the clock in the Clock Bar was a good few
    minutes fast:
A fiction no one really bothered to maintain, unlike
    the story
The comrade on my left was telling, which no one knew
    for certain truth:
*Back in 1922 a sergeant, I forget his name, was shot outside the*
    *National Bank …*
Ah yes, what year was it that they knocked it down? Yet, its
    memory's as fresh
As the inky smell of new pound notes – which interferes with
    the beer-and-whiskey
Tang of now, like two dogs meeting in the revolutionary 69
    of a long sniff,
Or cattle jostling shit-stained flanks in the Pound. For *pound,*
    as some wag
Interrupted, was an off-shoot of the Falls, from the Irish, *fál,*
    a hedge;
Hence, *any kind of enclosed thing,* its twigs and branches
    commemorated
By the soldiers' drab and olive camouflage, as they try to melt
Into a brick wall; red coats might be better, after all. *At*
    *any rate,*
*This sergeant's number came up; not a winning one. The bullet*
    *had his name on it.*

68

Though Sergeant X, as we'll call him, doesn't really feature
    in the story:
The nub of it is, *This tin can which was heard that night,*
    *trundling down*
*From the bank, down Balaclava Street. Which thousands heard,*
    *and no one ever*
*Saw. Which was heard for years, any night that trouble might be*
*Round the corner* ... and when it skittered to a halt, you knew
That someone else had snuffed it: a name drifting like an
    afterthought,
A scribbled wisp of smoke you try and grasp, as it becomes
    diminuendo, then
Vanishes. For *fál* is also *frontier, boundary,* as in *the*
    *undiscovered country*
*From whose bourne no traveller returns,* the illegible, thorny
    hedge of time itself –
Heartstopping moments, measured not by the pulse of a
    wristwatch, nor
The archaic anarchists' alarm-clock, but a mercury tilt device
Which 'only connects' on any given bump on the road. So,
    by this wingèd messenger
The promise 'to pay the bearer' is fulfilled:

As someone buys another round, an Allied Irish Banks
    £10 note drowns in
The slops of the counter; a Guinness stain blooms on the
    artist's impression
Of the sinking of the *Girona;* a tiny foam hisses round the
    salamander brooch
Dredged up to show how love and money endure, beyond
    death and the Armada,

Like the bomb-disposal expert in his suit of
    salamander-cloth.
Shielded against the blast of time by a strangely
    medieval visor,
He's been outmoded by this jerky robot whose various
    attachments include
*A large hook for turning over corpses that may be booby-trapped;*
But I still have this picture of his hands held up to avert
    the future
In a final act of *No surrender*, as, twisting through the
    murky fathoms
Of what might have been, he is washed ashore as pearl
    and coral.


This *strange eruption to our state* is seen in other versions of
    the Falls:
*A no-go area, a ghetto, a demolition zone.* For the ghost, as
    it turns out –
All this according to your man, and I can well believe it –
    this tin ghost,
Since the streets it haunted were abolished, was never
    heard again.
The sleeve of Raglan Street has been unravelled; the helmet
    of Balaclava
Is torn away from the mouth. The dim glow of Garnet has
    gone out,
And with it, all but the memory of where I lived. I, too,
    heard the ghost:
A roulette trickle, or the hesitant annunciation of a
    downpour, ricocheting
Off the window; a goods train shunting distantly into a
    siding,

Then groaning to a halt; the rainy cries of children after
    dusk.
For the voice from the grave reverberates in others' mouths,
    as the sails
Of the whitethorn hedge swell up in a little breeze,
    and tremble
Like the spiral blossom of Andromeda: so suddenly are
    shrouds and branches
Hung with street-lights, celebrating all that's lost, as fields
    are reclaimed
By the Starry Plough. So we name the constellations, to put
    a shape
On what was there; so, the storyteller picks his way between
    the isolated stars.

But, *Was it really like that?* And, *Is the story true?*
You might as well tear off the iron mask, and find that no
    one, after all,
Is there: nothing but a cry, a summons, clanking out from
    the smoke
Of demolition. Like some son looking for his father, or the
    father for his son,
We try to piece together the exploded fragments. Let these
    broken spars
Stand for the Armada and its proud full sails, for even if
The clock is put to rights, everyone will still believe it's fast:
The barman's shouts of *time* will be ignored in any case,
    since time
Is conversation; it is the hedge that flits incessantly into
    the present,
As words blossom from the drinkers' mouths, and the flotilla
    returns to harbour,
Long after hours.

Suddenly as the riot squad moved in, it was raining
    exclamation marks,
Nuts, bolts, nails, car keys. A fount of broken type. And
    the explosion
Itself – an asterisk on the map. This hyphenated line, a
    burst of rapid fire …
I was trying to complete a sentence in my head, but it
    kept stuttering,
All the alleyways and side streets blocked with stops
    and colons.

I know this labyrinth so well – Balaclava, Raglan, Inkerman,
    Odessa Street –
Why can't I escape? Every move is punctuated. Crimea Street.
    Dead end again.
A Saracen, Kremlin-2 mesh. Makrolon face-shields. Walkie-
    talkies. What is
My name? Where am I coming from? Where am I going? A
    fusillade of question marks.

# MEDBH McGUCKIAN
## b.1950

### TULIPS

Touching the tulips was a shyness
I had had for a long time – such
Defensive mechanisms to frustrate the rain
That shakes into the sherry glass
Of the daffodil, though scarcely
Love's young dream; such present-mindedness
To double-lock in tiers as whistle-tight,
Or catch up on sleep with cantilevered
Palms cupping elbows. It's their independence
Tempts them to this grocery of soul.

Except, like all governesses, easily
Carried away, in sunny
Absences of mirrors they exalt themselves
To ballets of revenge, a kind
Of twinness, an olympic way of earning,
And are sacrificed to plot, their faces
Lifted many times to the artistry of light –
Its lovelessness a deeper sort
Of illness than the womanliness
Of tulips with their bee-dark hearts.

## THE SITTING

My half-sister comes to me to be painted:
She is posing furtively, like a letter being
Pushed under a door, making a tunnel with her
Hands over her dull-rose dress. Yet her coppery
Head is as bright as a net of lemons, I am
Painting it hair by hair as if she had not
Disowned it, or forsaken those unsparkling
Eyes as blue may be sifted from the surface

Of a cloud; and she questions my brisk
Brushwork, the note of positive red
In the kissed mouth I have given her,
As a woman's touch makes curtains blossom
Permanently in a house: she calls it
Wishfulness, the failure of the tampering rain
To go right into the mountain, she prefers
My sea-studies, and will not sit for me
Again, something half-opened, rarer
Than railroads, a soiled red-letter day.

# PAUL MULDOON
## b.1951

### TRUCE

It begins with one or two soldiers
And one or two following
With hampers over their shoulders.
They might be off wildfowling

As they would another Christmas Day,
So gingerly they pick their steps.
No one seems sure of what to do.
All stop when one stops.

A fire gets lit. Some spread
Their greatcoats on the frozen ground.
Polish vodka, fruit and bread
Are broken out and passed round.

The air of an old German song,
The rules of Patience, are the secrets
They'll share before long.
They draw on their last cigarettes

As Friday-night lovers, when it's over,
Might get up from their mattresses
To congratulate each other
And exchange names and addresses.

# GREEN GOWN

In the afternoon my wife and I had a little quarrel which
I reconciled with a flourish. Then she read a sermon in
Dr Tillotson to me. It is to be observed that the flourish
was performed on the billiard table.

WILLIAM BYRD, diary entry for 30 July, 1710

Again and again, when it came her turn
to take a shot,
Marie's first inclination had been to pass
for she knew full well that as soon as she bent low
over the table I would draw
closer to glimpse her 'two young roes

that were twins' and the 'ivory
tower' of her neck and shoulder and side
and the small of her back
and maybe even the flat
of her belly ... 'The poets of *Sir Gawayne
and the Grene*

*Knight* and *The Romance of the Rose*

were among those whom Spenser would turn
and upon whom he would draw ...'
It was the week after the Aldershot
bomb and we were all lying low
for fear of reprisals from Donegall Pass

and Sandy Row ...'The description of a "greene
gowne" sported by Lecherie in *The Faerie Queene*,

for example ...' That vodka on the side
gave my glass of Heineken, which had fallen flat,
a little bit of pep ... Knock it back ...

Knock it back, Rainer, till you pass
out on a breast dripping Liebfraumilch or Mateus Rosé
or Hirondelle ... 'If John Livingston Lowes
is to be believed, Coleridge's turn
of mind was that of a man who's half-shot
most of the time ...' The main draw-

back,
then, of her house on College Green
had been that it was indeed a house, not a flat,
so that a gay Lothario
had to contend with the snide asides
of her Derry duennas ... Again and again

Dolores and Perpetua would gallop down a draw
and cut me off at the pass ...
Again and again I'd been shot
down in flames ... Until this evening, when I rose
to find my Princess Marie von Thurn
und Taxis-Hohenlohe

sitting on the stately pile of old issues of *Gown*
they used, I'm quite sure, for wiping their back-
sides,
tipping a bottle of green
stuff on to her left palm ...'Be it Fauré's
*Andante for Violin and Piano in B flat*

or his *Au bord de l'eau*,
his music fills me with longing …' You must draw
your own conclusions as to why things took this turn
after a month-long impasse,
but I suspect that I rose
in her estimation that afternoon when shot

after shot had rung out from Divis Flats
and I kept right on drinking my glass of Heineken
in the public bar of Lavery's
as if this was nothing more than a car back-
firing … In any event, I was slumped, green
at the gills, over the side

of the toilet bowl, when she shot
me a glance such as Daphne might shoot Apollo:
'We must gather the Rose
of love, whilst yet is time.' 'Time?' 'To withdraw …'
It had already given her a little pizzazz,
that vodka, emboldened her to turn

the cue, hard, as she struck the ball, lending it such side
that it hurtled across the bogs, fens, flats
of chalky green
all the way from Aquinas to (if I may) Quine
at whom it baulked, wheehee, did some class of a back-
flip, then rebounded off Porphyry

and Averroes … 'I use "withdraw"
in the Marvellian sense …' Spermicide, was it, or
    aloe vera?

'You'll be lucky to get an "allowed pass"…'
She lay on the flat of her back
in a haze of shot silk … 'Since you've not done a hand's
    turn …'
Her breast … 'Not a stroke …' The green of her
    green gown.

# LEON MCAULEY
## b.1952


## THE CHILDREN OF LIR

I claim as my own special property
the legend of *The Children of Lir*.
I guard it with some jealousy.
I stake my claim by vir-
tue of the incontrovertible fact
that I was brought up in Cushendall
on the shore of the North Channel
which was, in the mists of antiquity
(which differ from contemporary mists
in almost every quality,
and in none more so than their mystery)
of course, the Sea of Moyle.

I can, therefore, speak with some authority
on every aspect of the swan.
I have sought out and made careful study
of the swan everywhere I could find one.
I have sat by the Six Mile Water
and the shores of Lough Neagh
and watched them walk on water, swim the air,
noting the set and disposition of each muscle
(not that these swans in their off-white reality
bear any but the slightest similarity
to those great white swans of legend).

Fionnuala, with her brothers, I aver it, she
would have spurned the titbits we
throw at these shadows from our crisp-bags
as we stand laughing with our children,
amazed at their burgeoning humanity,
savouring their accuracy, their dexterity.
Largely we ignore the swans. Posterity
will not easily forgive us. It stands accusingly
even now and stares with its empty crisp-bag.
I have become expert, too, concerning chains.

Though my wife originates from Silverbridge
and therefore her native myth
and orthodoxy, for what it's worth
is the comings and goings
and to-ings and fro-ings
of the Gap of the North,
she is a Lirite too, taking to the faith,
as I often say, like a swan to water.
We have two sons and a daughter

and while we now live in Ballymena,
they have been brought up strict Lirites.
Indeed Fionnuala – that's my daughter's name –
sits up late into the night with me, discussing chains.
We find, in chains, an uncanny relevance
to contemporary life. We are convinced
that this is not simply coincidence or mere chance.
Distance, for example, is measured out in 'chains':
people speak of 'chains' of atoms – 'chains' of events.

But we have our enemies. We are an enclave
of Lirites trapped between the mad Sweeneys,
the Sons of Uisneach and the followers of Medbh.
They purport to despise us and lose no opportunity
to cast aspersions, if nothing worse.
'How can you be a Lirite, you, born in Dungannon?'
which I must admit is true – 'For heaven's sake
your father's from Glenravel!'
True again. But I have my answer:
for I am a Child of Lir –
and we were born to travel.

# RUTH CARR

## b.1953

### THE BLUE BOWL

*for Peter*

A go-between,
a traveller between hands,
a sacred proof of the journey
from me to you.
Caught in the cusp of china blue seas
we are waltzing on water,
embraced in this bowl
that opens its heart
like a miracle,
we carry and do not spill.

# C.L. DALLAT
## b.1953


### MORNING STAR

Only the half-asleep trucks
under sodium lights in the dockyard
see the MV *Matutina*
arrive under mercury floods;
the ramp hits the deck and they march,
this cohort of merchant marine,
verdigris buttons and flashes
of this or that long-defunct line,
those with no more than a brown-
paper parcel, some with kitbags
of laundry and presents and mounted
chronometers given in token
of unfinished decades of service
and each takes his taxi – a Humber,
or Wolseley, Granada or Zephyr
according to when each one last
saw shore leave, for nothing must seem
out-of-place on this homecoming dawn.

But as they take separate journeys
to sundry hill-farms in the glens
or one or another gaunt sandstone-
faced bay-window house by the shore
with its plaque in Fijian or Gaelic

84

no curtains are moved to watch out for
the taxi-lights rounding the point.

The lounge bars and chapels are dark
where they then were infrequent and ill-
at-ease guests, in silence the yards
where collies would once have held forth
bringing half-awake households to doors
but the front parlours still have kept faith
with their oak and mahogany sideboards
and paper-knives brought from Archangel,
Caracas, Vancouver, and they take
from the dresser the marquetry frame
with flesh tints and watered-green eyes
and they fumble for pipes in a drawer
and shaving-kits gilt with initials
and settle by various windows
to gaze at the light on the Mull,
the sidereal chart and the port-beams
of trawlers that drew them away.

And inside locked gates amid cypress,
names that were added as footnotes
to family stones are effaced
and on more-than-one high leaded-light,
a lacuna in glass is embraced
by the words OF YOUR CHARITY PRAY
FOR THE SOUL OF          LOST AT SEA.

# JANICE FITZPATRICK SIMMONS
## b.1954


### SALT CARESS

Once, on a sand bar, I saw a dying whale.
I asked you, father, if it was my whale,
the imaginary one that kept me company on the boat
during the long hours between catches.
*No*, you said. *Your whale will live a long time yet.*

How could I have imagined this loss:
me standing over my beloved's grave in the wind
that blows off the Atlantic visible from this
    Killult churchyard –
that same body of water throwing its salt caress
    over you too father,
buried in that land of childhood five thousands miles away?

The lap of water and the call of seabirds
in the salt-laden air are sunk deep in me.
When I walk by the sea – where I am walking
here and now, there and then – the ancient
light of stars still beating down on me.

I am trying to imagine a way out of this pain.
The whale is not dead yet. I can see its dorsal fin
crack the winter water's toss – it has its own journey
    to make.

# TESS HURSON
## b.1955


### RITE OF SPRING
#### *for my mother*

There is something growing in the way we talk;
As politicians tuning for their echo
Flick out keynotes,
Frisk, in their handshake, your visceral tic.
So much rides on the right innuendo
Our matched reflection in the rising well.

And in advancing we hear the jagged past,
The bull's memory of the china shop.
They are painting the bookie's for a spring touch-up,
We are wishing beyond all calculation.
Punters lay mayflowers at the outhouse doors
To charm off ill luck.

# CHRIS AGEE
## b.1956


### MUSHROOMING

Nothing stills the woods to silence
like the aftermath of rains, the meadow-crickets
    quenched,
the boughs and saplings of birch and pine

dropping their desultory *plops,* shining
here and there with sunshafts from parted cloud
whose mottle on moist leaf-litter

is a moss of light. This is the inspired time
the Greeks felt the mystery of Zeus,
the lightning's muse

in the dark labour of fungi. Vicarious as the uprush
of poetry, the delicate caps of mushrooms
thrust through the earth's rot, half-masked by a
    layer of leaves,

by mossy vestiges of treetrunks
holed by woodpeckers,
birch-logs broken-backed like tumbled pillars of alabaster,

branches fallen in autumn
where Indian pipe sprouts on bark
and a meandering wall is Frost's art

like lichen on the stones of Nineveh. A paradise of phalloi
mushrooming in damp, all named and infused
by the genius of fieldwork,

in the Eden of amateur mycology:
*Chanterelle, Thimble-cap, Velvet-footed Pax,*
the ochre, Latinate splendour

of *Voluminous Milky*
with its fishstink and profusion of latex:
each under-cap a haven for slugs,

a language all its own,
neither prose nor song,
not animal, yet not quite plant,

their svelte ethereal flesh
and tinges of extraordinary colour
the Zen of life,

a quickening blush of humus
in one-day miracles of the world's design
like haikus in the woodland epic of birth and decay.

# JEAN BLEAKNEY
## b.1956


## BY STARLIGHT ON NARIN STRAND

On a hot summer night, heavy with stars,
I am standing on the beach, stiff-necked,
watching for Perseids which, depending
on their size and angle of impact,
skate long tangents of brightness
or disintegrate in a short broad fizz of light.

During the gaps between Perseids, I think
of Claudius Ptolemaeus, the geographer
who, having mapped the ancient world,
tired of latitude and longitude and turned instead
to the wheels-within-wheels of the planets
and the fixed sphere of stars;

and how, noting the positions and magnitudes
of one thousand and twenty-eight stars,
he reached back across three millennia
to Babylon for the *Scorpion* and the *Bull;*
and humbly kept faith with the gods
in his naming of forty-eight constellations.

What pitch of darkness did he find
for such geometries? Did he travel,
by merchant ship to Ephesus or Antioch,

in order to pare down the horizon
and escape those mirrored fires –
the beams of the lighthouse at Alexandria?

Was he haunted by the frailty of night-vision
– how, when viewed directly, even the brightest star
diminishes? Did he think it mere illusion
or a god's conceit that leaves us trapped
like eternal nightwatchmen constantly scanning
the between-blackness of starlight?

This is what I am thinking about
at the hottest August of the century
on the darkest edge of the continent
as, during the intervals between Perseids
and the afterglow of spent wishes,
I faithfully retrace Ptolemy's dot-to-dot.

# MOYRA DONALDSON
## b.1956

### WORDS FROM THE OTHER SIDE

I visited my friend in hospital,
the day after she had died
and been brought back.
Her heart had stopped, exhausted
by another asthma attack,
by years of pumping
for an easy breath –
kicked back to life only
by doctors and electricity.

The air around her crackled.

Urgently
she pulled me close,
kissed my lips, placed
into the cave of my mouth,
onto my tongue
a message for me, carried back –

*death's easy* – she said –
*much easier than life*

and her words hit me
like an amphetamine rush,
dizzied me, left me
electrified, unsure
if I'd been given
a blessing or a curse.

# CATHAL Ó SEARCAIGH
## b.1956

### DO ISAAC ROSENBERG

Le bánú an lae agus muid ag teacht ar ais
i ndiaidh a bheith ag suirí i mbéal an uaignis
d'éirigh na fuiseoga as poill agus prochóga Phrochlais

agus chuimhnigh mé ortsa, a Isaac Rosenberg,
cathshuaite i dtailte treascartha na Fraince, ag éisteacht
le ceol sítheach na bhfuiseog le teacht an lae

agus tú ag pilleadh ar do champa, thar chnámha créachta
do chairde, ruaithne reatha na bpléascán, creathánach,
ag deargadh an dorchadais ar pháirc an chatha.

Ag éisteacht le meidhir na bhfuiseog idir aer agus uisce
thaibhsigh do dhánta chugam thar thalamh eadrána na
        síoraíochta, líne,
ar líne, stadach, scáfar mar shaighdiúirí ó bhéal an áir

agus bhain siad an gus asam lena gcuntas ar an Uafás
as duibheagán dubh na dtrinsí, as dóchas daortha na n-óg,
        as ár
agus anbhás, d'éirigh siad chugam as corrabhuais coinsiasa –

mise nach raibh ariamh sa bhearna bhaoil, nach dtug
ruathar mharfach thar an mhullach isteach sa chreach,
nár fhulaing i dtreascairt dhian na fola;

nach bhfaca saighdiúirí óga mar bheadh sopóga ann, caite
i gcuibhrinn mhéith an áir, boladh bréan an bháis
ag éirí ina phláigh ó bhláth feoite a n-óige;

nach raibh ar maos i nglár is i gclábar bhlár an chatha,
nár chaill mo mheabhair i bpléasc, nár mhothaigh an piléar
mar bheach thapaidh the ag diúl mhil fhiáin m'óige.

Ó ná hagair orm é, a Isaac Rosenberg, d'ainm a lua,
mise atá díonaithe i mo dhánta i ndún seo na Seirce
agus creach dhearg an chogaidh i gcroí na hEorpa go fóill.

Ach bhí mo chroí lasta le lúcháir agus caomhchruth álainn
mo leannán le mo thaobh, gach géag, gach alt, gach rinn,
gach ball de na ballaibh ó mhullach go talamh mo
    mhealladh,

sa chruth go gcreidim agus muid i mbachlainn a chéile
go bhfuil díon againn ar bhaol, go bhfuil an saol lán d'fhéile,
go bhfuil amhrán ár ngrá ina gheas ar gach aighneas.

Agus tá na fuiseoga ag rá an rud céanna liomsa a dúirt
    siad leatsa
sular cuireadh san aer tú, sular réabadh do chnámha –
Is fearr cumann agus ceol ná cogadh agus creach;

agus cé nach raibh mé ariamh i mbéal an chatha
agus cé nach bhfuil caite agam ach saol beag suarach,
    sabháilte,
ag daingniú mo choirnéil féin agus ag cúlú ó chúiseanna
    reatha;

ba mhaith liom a dhearbhú duitse, a fhile, a d'fhán go
   diongbháilte
i mbun d'fhocail, a labhair le lomchnámh na fírinne ó ár
   an chatha –
go bhfuil mise fosta ar thaobh an tSolais, fosta ar thaobh
   na Beatha.

## FOR ISAAC ROSENBERG

At dawn, we gave up our courting
out in the wilderness. Larks soared
from the bog-holes and hollows of Prochlais.

Then I thought of you, Isaac Rosenberg,
war-weary in the 'torn fields of France',
stunned by the siren larks, one dawn

as you returned to your camp over the ruined
bones of friends, shaken, with bombs
pouncing on the red and black battlefield.

The larks' joy between air and water
brought your poems across eternity's barricade, line
by line, stutteringly, scared, like soldiers in battle,

and they stopped me in my tracks with horror:
the dark pits of trenches, youth's smashed-up
hopes, the carnage wracked my conscience,

I who was never within an ounce of my life,
who never had to pile over the top and into battle,
who never lost out in any of the bloodshed,

I who never saw young soldiers torched
and dumped in an open field of slaughter,
their blighted bodies stinking with death,

I who was never plunged in the mud and mire,
never shell-shocked or stung by a bullet
sucking out my life like some crazy bee honey ...

O, don't mind me, Isaac Rosenberg, calling you
from here, my safe-house of love poems,
while Europe still eats its heart out;

only mine was light with joy, my lover
beside me in all his glory, every limb,
joint, rim, every bit of him tempting me

to believe that we're safe together,
that life is for feasting
and love wards off trouble.

The larks tell me what they told you,
before you were blown to pieces –
that love and music beat war and empire;

and though I've never been in action,
though I've had a safe, ordinary life,
looking after my own and keeping out of it,

I want to assure you, poet whose truth
was bared to the bones in World War I,
I too am on the side of light, and of life.

*translated from the Irish by Frank Sewell*

## I gCEANN MO THRÍ BLIANA A BHÍ MÉ
*do Anraí Mac Giolla Chomhaill*

'Sin clábar! Clábar cáidheach,
a chuilcigh,' a dúirt m'athair go bagrach
agus mé ag slupairt go súgach
i ndíobhóg os cionn an bhóthair.
'Amach leat as do chuid clábair
sula ndéanfar tú a chlonáil!'

Ach choinnigh mé ag spágáil agus ag splaiseáil
agus ag scairtigh le lúcháir:
'Clábar! Clábar! Seo mo chuid clábair!'
Cé nár chiallaigh an focal faic i mo mheabhair
go dtí gur mhothaigh mé i mo bhuataisí glugar
agus trí gach uile líbín de mo cheirteacha
creathanna fuachta na tuisceana.

A chlábar na cinniúna, bháigh tú mo chnámha.

99

CLABBER: THE POET AT THREE YEARS

'That's clabber! Clutching clabber
sucks caddies down,' said my father harshly
while I was stomping happily
in the ditch on the side of the road.
'Climb out of that clabber pit
before you catch your death of it!'

But I went on splattering and splashing,
and scattering whoops of joy:
'Clabber! Clabber! I belong to it,'
although the word meant nothing to me
until I heard a squelch in my wellies
and felt through every fibre of my duds
the cold tremors of awakening knowledge.

O elected clabber, you chilled me to the bone.

*translation from the Irish by John Montague*

# ANDREW ELLIOTT
## b.1961

### ANGEL

I think to make love to a nurse would be perfect,
Every germ and virus swimming in her mind
Like a kaleidoscope moving

Under a patient's skin,
Her breasts having nightmares of cancer,
Her hands like bowls weighing the ghosts of diseases.

Because she cannot control what she sees
Her body has turned inside out in the way she talks,
And left me, like a willing unfortunate,

To make my love nest
Among imaginary glands
And strange passageways,

The pink and white tissues of her genitals;
Unvaccinated and tempting fate
By bedding down with the untouchables,

Loving everything that happens under her skin.

# JOHN HUGHES
## b.1962


## A RESPECT FOR LAW AND ORDER
### *for Dermot Seymour*

The general will be shot in the face
when his new chauffeur forgets orders
and stops for a red traffic-light.
Within the hour one of the usual suspects
will be rounded up and taken downtown
to an interrogation room on the tenth floor
of the National Central Security building;
and after five hours of electric shocks
and beatings with a length of rubber-hose
he will be ordered to open the window
and step outside for a breath of fresh air.

He will fall head-first onto a crowded pavement
of journalists, pickpockets, private detectives,
air-force pilots, French polishers, jazz-guitarists,
civil servants in the Department of Information,
elderly women on their way across town
to visit their latest grandchild,
young men sauntering to a soccer match
between the national side and Paraguay,
a famous Italian new expressionist painter,
and the newly-arrived cultural attaché
of the Republic of South Africa.

The suspect will then pick himself up,
take a look at himself in the nearest window,
tuck in his shirt, straighten his tie,
and disappear into the leafy suburb
where he lives in a modest apartment
with his second wife and her two children;
and finish the book he was reading
when interrupted by an old schoolfriend
dressed to the nines in a uniform
he had recently come to respect.

# DAMIAN SMYTH

## b.1962

### DISAPPEARED

Along the border, where x marks the spot,
the bodies have moulted from the black bin bags
that did them as shrouds in the hurry of night.

Now at Rossglass the seals break the surface,
the souls of the dead peering sadly ashore,
balaclavas of pelt pulled tight on their skulls.

# MARTIN MOONEY
## b.1964


## FOOTBALLERS IN THE SNOW

The dark comes early now on Saturdays.
Under the aurorae of the floodlights'
huge radiant dice, the teams' jerseys glow
like a kid's painting, and the luminous

raincoats of the police on crowd-control
are warm as pub windows. But overhead
a polar winter exhales. Its breath
and its long night, its powercut, sweep south.

The first flurry of snow blows in as if
the planet had lurched like a drunk on ice.
The fans blur on the opposite terrace.
The linesman evaporates on his line.

The yellow cops, the footballers in red
and blue, waver, diminish and recede.
The vast pitch whitens under the flakes thrown
sideways into the stadium. The goals

are swallowed up by light years of bleached ground.
It's as if some impatient cosmic
law (of entropy, say) had raised its hand.
As if the world's end was in this last glimpse

of twenty-two men in colourless shirts
and a single figure in black, who stops
in the faint tracks he has just noticed
and raises a whistle to his lips.

# KATE NEWMANN

## b.1965

### DREAM OF A PORTRAIT PAINTER ON A SUNDAY AFTERNOON IN THE ALAMEDA

*for Ben and Anna*

I am failing him, I know
From the people who stop to stare.
He makes me look straight at him.
We are an arm's length apart
In his booth.
His face creases to an intricate grid
Moving to map my features.
I can see backwards
Through his plain glass glasses,
Thick black frames
Worn, like Martin Luther King's,
From need to give his vision weight
In the eyes of the world.
I sense sadness settle on my face.
He grapples in his pocket,
Rubs out the last line.
All his money is in his sock.
He gives me my change,
Says I am like a saint,
Crossing himself, signs his name, Flores,
And hands me my portrait
Of someone else.

# PÓL Ó MUIRÍ

## b.1965

### BOBBY, WILFRED AND SEÁN

In fifth-year we met
Wilfred Owen, Seán O'Casey and Bobby Sands.
Our English teacher did his best
To show us that Wilfred and Seán were right:
*Ah, lads,* Dulce et decorum est. *It isn't true.*
But Bobby Sands was after dying
And we weren't too sure.
In the theatre, the volunteer said:
*Boyle, no man can do enough for Ireland.*
We let out a roar which lifted the rafters
Just to let the Protestant schools know
That we were there, that we had risen from our knees
Now and forever.
Poor Wilfred.
How could we listen to him
While coffin after coffin trailed
Down the trenches of our streets?
Poor O'Casey.
We thought that the volunteer had it right –
Johnny Boyle was nothing but
A waster of a traitor.
We were the hard men those days.

# DEIRDRE CARTMILL
## b.1967

### THE WATERFALL WALK

It was a row that brought us here.
As if to prove you care
you place your fingers in the small of my back,
ease me off the wooden bench.
We lean over the railings, let the cold spray
spatter our faces and you point out the way
the waterfall mutates when you stare
at its fractured face. The surface allure
obscures the struggle
which fuels its forward surge,
fierce after rain, gentler in the sun,
an eternal momentum
that feeds on the give and take.
I turn and kiss your wet face.

# MAIRTÍN CRAWFORD
## 1967–2004


### UNTITLED SONNET

What are we looking for all these years?
It can't be far from us though seasons change
light's sensuous quality and our perceptions
alter irrevocably. Like autumn sunlight
its colder glance reminds us that there's
more to life than summers of indolent repose.
What we have we cannot help but lose.
None of it can go on forever.

But behind winter there's always spring.
You can't go on in silence imagining
the pure idea of silence. Look out
your window. The trees are waving in
unison because the dead are returning
to us, reborn, in new, perfect forms.

# GEARÓID MAC LOCHLAINN
## b.1967


## AN MÁINE GAELACH
### *do m'athair*

Ba ghnách linn dul le m'athair,
ar mhaidneacha Sathairn
sula mbíodh na tábhairní oscailte,
chuig siopaí peataí deannacha Shráid Ghréisim.
Uaimheanna dorcha iontais,
an t-aer tiubh le mún is min sáibh
a chuirfeadh na poill sróine ag rince.
Ní bhíodh le cloisteáil istigh
ach fuaim shúilíní ciúine uisce,
glúp ruball éisc
ag tumadh go bun babhla
ag radharc ina mionlongbhá rúnda,
seabhrán sciatháin cholmáin shnoite.
Brioscarnach mhistéireach
i measc an fhéir thirim bhuí.
Bhíodh hamstair, geirbilí, luchóga bána
coiníní dubha, pearaicítí buí,
nathracha malltriallacha ina gcodladh céad bliain
mar a bheadh an áit faoi dhraíocht.
Bhíodh an toirtís bhrónach
ag síorgheimhriú,
corntha ina blaosc mhurtallach,
dubh dóite le méara tanaí páisti
ag priocadh ghreille a cáis ghruama.

111

Ach ba chuma linn
faoin chuibhreann Andaithe Falsa Seo
fad is a bhí seisean ann
ag amharc anuas, ó phriocaire te a phéirse
ar an domhan marbh geimhrúil seo,
ag preabadach ó chos go cos
ina chulaith dhúchleiteach chorraithe.
Pótaire de shagart ar a phuilpid,
Áhab ag stiúradh choite an tsiopa
lena chuid bladhmaireachta boirbe.
Mothaím go fóill
a shúil mhire shoiléir
ar casadh ina cheann slíoctha,
mar mhirlín dubh
ag tolladh chúl mo chinn,
ag gliúcaíocht orm,
a ghnúis aosta claonta ar leataobh.
Éan corr, mheall sé lena ghlórtha muid,
snagaire de sheanchaí sraoilleach,
a bhéal ar maos le mallachtaí meisceoirí,
eascainí graosta,
focal faire na nÓglach
ó bhallaí Bhóthar na bhFál.
Aisteoir teipthe ag aithris
reitric fholamh na sráide dúinn,
téad ar a chos a cheangail é le
bata scóir a phéirse –
Suibhne ceangailte is cuachta
lena mhearadh focal.

Rinne muid ceap magaidh den gheabaire gaoithe seo
is a fhoclóir cúng sráide,
chuir muid maslaí ar ár n-óráidí tragóideach
is d'fhág muid ár gcuid filíochta slapaí
ar a theanga bhocht bhriste
a bhí líofa tráth
le grág is cá.

THE IRISH-SPEAKING MYNAH

*for my father*

Saturday mornings
before pub opening time
my father would take us
to the pet-shops in Gresham Street –
dark Aladdin's caves
reeking of piss and sawdust.
All you could hear in there
was bubbles
or the bloop of a goldfish
diving to the seabed
of its glass world
where it hid behind a pebble,
or a dove gobbling
at its wing feathers
amid a bed of golden crackling straw.
Hamsters, gerbils, white mice,
black bunnies, and canary birds,
sleeping-beauty-serpents;
the melancholy tortoise
in eternal hibernation,
a Rip Van Winkle
fed-up with the grubby mits of kids
poking at it through the wire grille.
But no matter about this fool's paradise
so long as *he* was there,
looking quizzically down from his perch
at the comatose world,
shifting from foot to foot

114

in his dazzling feather boa outfit,
a whiskey-priest in the pulpit,
Ahab steering the pet-shop to perdition
from a crow's nest of rant.

I can still see him
jooking at me with his head cocked
to one side,
his mad eye
rolling like a buller in its socket,
boring into the back of my skull.
Quixotic bird, tattered old sea-dog,
he stammered out amazing repartee
and drunken troopers' curses,
all the passwords of the old Falls Road IRA.
Resting actor, stuck to the barstool
of his perch, a veritable Sweeney
tethered by his string of gabble.

We made a laughing stock of this old windbag,
mocked his down-town word-store.
We'd no time for fancy grave orations
so we thrust our sloppy poetry
on his tragic tongue
that was once fluent
with squawk and caw.

*translated from the Irish by Ciaran Carson*

# SINEAD MORRISSEY
## b.1972


### SEA STONES

It is exactly a year today since you slapped me in public.
I took it standing up. You claimed I just ignored it,
that I pretended to be hooked on the dumb-show of a sunset,
splashing, a mile off. Too hooked to register
the sting of your ring finger
as it caught on my mouth and brought my skin with it.

All the next day I rolled with a migraine
down a merciless gallery that was mercifully without sun.
Sloshed tea in the saucer when your name came up.
I couldn't stop the cup of my hurt
flowing over and over until I saw there was no end of it
and only an end to me. How promiscuous pain can be.

He gave me roses. The surprise of butterflies caged in
     the palms.
And sea stones with tracings of juvenile kisses, scented
     with risk.
I wrapped them in black at the back of a bottom drawer,
hidden in underwear. The truth – that you never were
     so vivid
or so huge as the second the street turned towards us
in shock – got dropped between us like a fallen match.

You turned away as the sun disappeared like a ship. And I,
suddenly wanting to be struck again, to keep the fire of
    your anger lit,
I bit my lip.

# CLOCKS

The sadness of their house is hard to defeat. There are at least
 three clocks per room.
There are two people with nothing to do but to be in each
 room and be separate.
The person each room was decorated by was seconded to a
 plot in a cemetery
that is walked to every day, and tended like a bedroom
 sanctuary. No notice given.


The clocks do all the talking. He visits the grave in the
 middle of a three-hour loop
and knows the year of completion of every castle in Ireland.
 His route
is always the same: the round tower via the aqueduct via the
 cemetery via the ramparts
via the Battle of Antrim during the Rising of the
 United Irishmen in 1798,
the slaughter of which is more present if he's deep in
 the morning
of his April wedding breakfast or locked into the moment
 they fitted the oxygen mask
and she rolled her bruised eyes back. She is unable to find the
 stop for the bus to Belfast
and stays indoors. The nets turn the daylight white and
 empty.
She has worn the married life of her sister so tightly
over her own, the noise of the clocks makes her feel almost
 without skin.
Sometimes she sits in her sister's chair, and feels guilty.

She has *Countdown* for company and a selective memory –
the argument at the funeral with her niece over jewellery
    and, years ago,
the conspiracy to keep her single, its success. Time settles
    over
    each afternoon
like an enormous wing, when the flurry of lunchtime has
    left them
and the plates have already been set for tea. He reads
    extensively –
from *Hitler and Stalin, Parallel Lives*, to *Why Ireland Starved* –
but has taken to giving books away recently to anyone
    who calls.
Winter or summer, evenings and early: they retire to their
    separate rooms
at least two hours before sleep. It falls like an act of mercy
when the twenty-two clocks chime eight o'clock in almost
    perfect unison.

# ALAN GILLIS

## b.1973

### 12TH OCTOBER, 1994

I enter the Twilight Zone,
    the one run
by Frankie 'Ten Pints' Fraser, and slide the heptagon
    of my twenty
pence piece into its slot. The lights come on.
    Sam the Sham
and the Pharaohs are playing 'Wooly Bully'.

A virtual combat zone lights up the green
    of my eyes,
my hand clammy on the joystick, as Johnny 'Book
    Keeper' McFeeter
saunters in and Smokey sings 'The Tracks of My Tears'.
    He gives the nod
to Betty behind the bulletproof screen.

Love of my life he says, and she says
    ach Johnny,
when who do you know but Terry 'The Blaster' McMaster
    levels in
and B Bumble and The Stingers start playing 'Nut Rocker'.
    I shoot down
a sniper and enter a higher level.

Betty buzzes Frankie who has a shifty
        look around,
poking his nut around a big blue door, through which
        I spy
Billy 'Warts' McBreeze drinking tea and tapping his toes
        to Randy
and The Rainbows' version of 'Denise'.

On the screen I mutilate a double-agent
    Ninja and collect
a bonus drum of kerosene. 'Game of Love' by Wayne
        Fontana pumps
out of the machine, when I have to catch my breath,
        realising Ricky
'Rottweiler' Rice is on my left

saying watch for the nifty fucker
        with the cross
bow on the right. Sweat-purls tease my spine, tensed ever
        more rigidly,
when Ricky's joined by Andy 'No Knees' Tweed,
        both of them
whistling merrily to The Crystals' 'Then He Kissed Me'.

What the fuck is going on
        here asks
Victor 'Steel Plate' Hogg, as he slides through the fire
        door. The kid's
on level 3, says Andy. At which point Frankie does his nut,
        especially since
The Cramps are playing 'Can your Pussy do the Dog?'

Betty puts on Curtis and the Clichés'
    'Brush Against Me
Barbarella' instead, when the first helicopter shreds the air
    to the left
of the screen. Gathering my wits and artillery, I might eclipse
    the high score
of Markie 'Life Sentence' Prentice, set on October 6th.

I hear Benny 'Vindaloo' McVeigh say
    right we're going
to do this fucking thing. By now the smoke is so thick
    the screen is almost grey.
The Shangri-Las are playing 'Remember (Walkin' in the Sand)'.
    Frankie Says
no, Victor, nobody's going to fucking disband.

Bob B Soxx and The Blue Jeans are playing
    'Zip-A-Dee-Doo-Dah'.
Through a napalm blur I set the interns free. They wear US
    marine khaki.
Jimmy 'Twelve Inch' Lynch says son, not bad for 20p.
    I leave the Zone and go
back to the fierce grey day. It looks like snow.

# LEONTIA FLYNN
## b.1974

## BY MY SKIN

*for Terry McGaughey*

Mr Bennet in *Pride and Prejudice – The Musical!*,
my father communicates with his family almost entirely
    through song.
From the orange linoleum and trumpet-sized wallpaper
    flowers
of the late 1970s, he steps with a roll of cotton,
a soft-shoe routine, and a pound of soft white paraffin.

He sings 'Oft in the Stilly Night' and 'Believe Me, If All
    Those Endearing Young Charms'.
He sings 'Edelweiss' and 'Cheek to Cheek' from *Top Hat*.
Disney animals are swaying along the formica sink-top
where he gets me into a lather. He greases behind my
    knees
and the folds of my elbows; he wraps me in swaddling
    clothes.

Then lifts me up with his famous high-shouldered shuffle
– 'Yes Sir, That's My Baby!' – to the candlewick bunk.
The air is bright with a billion exfoliate flitters
as he changes track – one for his changeling child:
'Hauld Up Your Head My Bonnie Wee Lass and Dinnae
    Look So Shy'.

123

He sings 'Put Your Shoes On, Lucy (Don't You Know
   You're In The City)'.
He sings 'Boolavogue' and 'Can't Help Loving that Man
   of Mine'
and 'Lily the Pink' and 'The Woods of Gortnamona'.
He sings – the lights are fading – 'Slievenamon'
and about the 'Boy Blue' (who awakens 'to angel song').

My father is Captain Von Trapp, Jean Valjean, Professor
   Henry Higgins –
gathering his repertoire, with the wheatgerm and
   cortisone,
like he's gathering up a dozen tribute roses.
Then, taking a bow, he lays these – just so – by my skin
which gets better and worse, and worse and better again.

# AFTERWORD

As I recall it, the Belfast Group of the late 1960s and early 70s was a somewhat loose group. True, it had formal meetings in the back room of Queen's English Department at 4 University Square, but it was really a moveable feast, and its members were just as likely to congregate over a few or many drinks in other venues that lay within a half-mile radius of the Lanyon Building – the Eg, the Bot, the Welly, the Arts Club, the Elbow Room, the Cobbles. It would have been in one or other of these places that I first got to know the likes of the poets Michael Longley, Seamus Heaney, Trevor McMahon, Robert Johnstone and Paul Muldoon, the prose writer Bernard MacLaverty, the painter and poet Jack Pakenham and the critic Michael Allen; later Medbh McGuckian and John Morrow. We would talk books, sport, politics, music, art and the weather. I think we were mutually supportive, but heavy slagging was also par for the course. It was the heyday of *The Honest Ulsterman*, under the aegis of Frank Ormsby, and many of us were first published in that magazine. It is appropriate and inevitable that Frank should be the editor of the present volume.

When I was appointed Director of the Seamus Heaney Centre for Poetry in 2003, it was one of my hopes that the Centre could recreate some of the aura of those heady days. I found that much of it was already there. The young poet and critic Alan Gillis had admirably managed the Centre before my arrival; the English Society, under the direction of Edna Longley, Fran Brearton and Eamonn Hughes, had of course been maintaining its brilliant series of readings over the years; another manifestation of the Group was being led by the poet Sinead Morrissey; the staff of the School of English included the writers Medbh McGuckian, Glenn Patterson and Daragh Carville; and poets of the calibre of Jean Bleakney and Leontia Flynn were about. When Paul Durcan, the present Ireland Professor of Poetry, came to spend a term in residence in the Centre in 2005, he commented that its warren of small rooms reminded him of an early Irish monastery: writers busy at their work like monks in their cells, as in the monastery of Bangor, one of whose scribes wrote the Blackbird poem that inspired the emblem of the Seamus Heaney Centre for Poetry and the title of this volume.

*The Blackbird's Nest* is tangible proof that poetry at Queen's University Belfast is alive and well; and I have no doubt that were a similar anthology to be compiled a generation from now, it would include a good deal many more poets than those represented here.

CIARAN CARSON

# BIOGRAPHICAL NOTES

CHRIS AGEE was born in 1956 in San Francisco and grew up in Massachusetts, New York and Rhode Island. He attended Harvard University and since 1979 has lived in Ireland. In 1985 he was awarded a PGCE by Queen's University Belfast and in 1987 an MA in Anglo-Irish Literature. He is the author of two collections of poems, *In the New Hampshire Woods* (1992) and *First Light* (2003), and edited *Scar on the Stone: Contemporary Poetry from Bosnia* (1998) and *Unfinished Ireland: Essays on Hubert Butler* (2003). He teaches at the Open University and edits *Irish Pages*, a journal of contemporary writing.

JEAN BLEAKNEY was born in Newry, County Down, in 1956 and educated at Newry High School and Wallace High School, Lisburn. She studied Biochemistry at Queen's University Belfast (1974–78) and worked at the University as a biochemist in medical research (1979–87). Later she attended workshops with Carol Rumens at Queen's. She has published two collections of poems: *The Ripple Tank Experiment* (1999) and *The Poet's Ivy* (2003). She currently works in a garden centre in Belfast.

JOHN CAMPBELL was born in 1936 in Belfast's York Street area. He worked at Belfast docks until 1985 and also served for a time as a security man at Queen's University Belfast. Now retired, he is still an active member of the Transport and General Workers' Union. His publications include three collections of poetry: *Saturday Night in York Street* (1982), *An Oul Jobbin' Poet* (1989) and *Memories of York Street* (1991), and a novel, *Corner Kingdom* (1999). *The Rose and Blade: New and Selected Poems 1957–1997* was published in 2005.

RUTH CARR was born in Belfast in 1953 and educated at Queen's University Belfast. A member of the Word of Mouth Poetry Collective, she has worked with local writers' groups and edited a number of anthologies, such as *The Female Line* (1985), the first anthology of poetry and fiction by Northern Irish women writers. She was associate editor of the *HU* poetry magazine. Her collection of poems, *There is a House,* was published in 1999.

CIARAN CARSON was born in Belfast in 1948 and educated at St Mary's Christian Brothers' School and Queen's University Belfast (1967–71). He worked for the Northern Ireland Civil Service, and for the Arts Council of Northern Ireland as Traditional Arts Officer and, later, Literature Officer. He has, to date, published four prose works and nine collections of poetry and has won several poetry awards, including the T.S. Eliot Prize for *First Language* (1993) and the Forward Prize for Best Collection for *Breaking News* (2003). His translation of Dante's *The Inferno* was published in 2002. He is the first Director of the Seamus Heaney Centre for Poetry at Queen's.

DEIRDRE CARTMILL was born in Moy, County Tyrone, in 1967. She graduated from Queen's University Belfast in 1989 with a degree in Electrical and Electronic Engineering and received an MA in Creative Writing from the University in 2002. She works as a script editor for the BBC and has published one collection of poems, *Midnight Solo* (2004).

MAIRTÍN CRAWFORD (1967–2004) was born in Belfast and educated at Queen's University Belfast, where he co-edited *Gown Literary Supplement* and *The Big Spoon*. He worked as a creative writing instructor, was a director of the Between the Lines literature festival, served as writer in residence at the Crescent Arts Centre and was a production editor with *Fortnight* magazine. He helped write the documentary film *Storm Bird*, about the poet Padraic Fiacc. His *Selected Poems* was published posthumously in 2005.

C.L. DALLAT was born in Ballycastle, County Antrim, in 1953 and studied Statistics and Operational Research at Queen's University Belfast. He has worked in publishing and information technology, and as a musician, critic and broadcaster. His collection of poems *Morning Star* was published in 1998.

SEAMUS DEANE was born in Derry in 1940 and educated at St Columb's College, Derry, Queen's University Belfast (1957–61) and Pembroke College, Cambridge (1963–66). He was Professor of Modern English and American Literature at University College Dublin (1980–93), before moving to the University of Notre Dame, Indiana, where he currently teaches. In addition to poetry, he has published several critical studies and was a member of the Field Day Theatre Company and general editor of *The Field Day Anthology of Irish Writing* (1991). His *Selected Poems* was published in 1988 and his novel *Reading in the Dark* was shortlisted for the Booker Prize in 1996.

MOYRA DONALDSON was born in Newtownards, County Down, in 1956 and educated at Glenlola Collegiate School, Queen's University Belfast (1975–79), where she studied English, and at the University of Ulster, where she did a postgraduate course in social work. She has published two collections of poems: *Snakeskin Stilettos* (1998) and *Beneath the Ice* (2001).

ANDREW ELLIOTT was born in Limavady, County Derry, in 1961, spent his early childhood in Banbridge, County Down, and attended Coleraine Academical Institution as a boarder. He studied for a year in Cardiff, then at Queen's University Belfast, graduating in 1984. In 1985 he was the first recipient of the Allan Dowling Poetry Travelling Fellowship. His collection *The Creationists* was published in 1988.

JAMES ELLIS was born in Belfast in 1931 and educated at Methodist College and Queen's University Belfast, where he read English, French and Philosophy. Later he attended the Bristol Old Vic Theatre School. He is best-known as a television actor but has also acted on stage with, for example, the Royal Shakespeare Company and has worked as a theatre director. His collection of poems *Domestic Flight* was published in 1998.

JAMES FENTON was born near Ballymoney, County Antrim, in 1931 and educated at Dalriada School, Ballymoney, and Stranmillis College (1965–69). In 1965 he took up part-time degree study at Queen's University Belfast, graduating in 1969. He was awarded a BSc in Economics in 1970. He spent his working life as a teacher in Belfast and was Principal of Ballysillan Primary School. He published *The Hamely Tongue* in 1995 (new edition, 2000), a record of contemporary Ulster-Scots, and his collection of Ulster-Scots poems, *Thonner An Thon*, appeared in 2000.

LEONTIA FLYNN was born in Downpatrick, County Down, in 1974 and educated at Queen's University Belfast and Edinburgh University, before returning to Queen's to write her doctoral thesis on the poetry of Medbh McGuckian. Her first collection of poems, *These Days* (2004), won the Whitbread Prize for Poetry and she was selected as one of the 2004 New Generation Poets.

MICHAEL FOLEY was born in Derry in 1947 and educated at St Columb's College, Derry, and Queen's University Belfast, where he obtained a BSc in Chemistry and an MSc in Computer Science. He was joint editor of *The Honest Ulsterman* magazine from 1969 to 1972. In addition to three novels, he has published four collections of poetry: *True Life Love Stories* (1976), *The GO Situation* (1982), *Insomnia in the Afternoon* (1994) and *Autumn Beguiles the Fatalist* (2006). He lectures in Information Technology at the University of Westminster.

ALAN GILLIS was born in Belfast in 1973. He completed his PhD at Queen's and worked at the Seamus Heaney Centre for Poetry from its inception. He is author of the critical work *Irish Poetry of the 1930s* and his collection of poems *Somebody, Somewhere* was published by Gallery Press in 2004. He is currently a lecturer in English at the University of Edinburgh.

ROBERT GREACEN was born in Derry in 1920 and grew up in Belfast, where he attended Methodist College. He continued his education at Queen's, where, with John Gallen, he edited the University's literary magazine, *The Northman*, and at Trinity College Dublin. He edited several anthologies of Ulster writing and (with Valentin Iremonger) *The Faber Book of Contemporary Irish Poetry* (1949). His autobiography *Even Without Irene* (1969) was re-issued in 1995. His *Collected Poems 1944–1994* (1995) won the Irish Times Literature Prize for Poetry.

W.J. HARVEY (1925–67) was Professor of English at Queen's University Belfast from 1965 to 1967 and attended meetings of Philip Hobsbaum's writers' group. He was well known as a critic of nineteenth- and twentieth-century fiction and poetry and published two collections of poems, *The Uncertain Margin* (1945) and *Exile and Return* (1948). *Descartes' Dream*, a chapbook of previously unpublished poems, with a preface by Seamus Heaney and a postscript by F.W. Bateson, was published in 1973.

SEAMUS HEANEY was born in County Derry in 1939 and educated at St Columb's College, Derry, and Queen's University Belfast (1957–61), where he was also a lecturer in English (1966–72). He has served as Boylston Professor of Rhetoric and Oratory at Harvard University and as Professor of Poetry at Oxford University, and won the Nobel Prize for Literature in 1995. He is currently Emerson Poet in Residence at Harvard. His many collections of poetry include *Opened Ground: Poems 1966–1996* (1998), *Electric Light* (2001) and *District and Circle* (2006). He is also a noted critic and translator. He received an honorary degree from Queen's in 1982. The University opened the Seamus Heaney Library in 1997 and the Seamus Heaney Centre for Poetry in 2003.

JOHN HEWITT (1907–87) was born in Belfast and educated at the Royal Belfast Academical Institution and Methodist College, Belfast. He attended Queen's from 1924 to 1930 and later worked as Assistant Curator of Art at the Belfast Museum and Art Gallery. From 1957 to 1972 he was Director of the Herbert Art Gallery in Coventry. He served as the first writer in residence at Queen's from 1976 to 1979 and was awarded an honorary degree by the University in 1983, the same year that he was made a freeman of the city of Belfast. The first annual John Hewitt International Summer School took place in 1988 and *The Collected Poems of John Hewitt*, edited by Frank Ormsby, was published in 1991.

PHILIP HOBSBAUM (1932–2005) was born in London and educated at Downing College, Cambridge, the Royal Academy of Music, London, and the University of Sheffield. He worked as a lecturer in English at Queen's University Belfast from 1962 to 1966, founding the influential writers' group which became a focus for a wide range of emerging poets and prose writers. Later he was appointed Titular Professor of English at the University of Glasgow. In addition to a number of critical works, he published four collections of poems: *The Place's Fault and Other Poems* (1964), *In Retreat and Other Poems* (1966), *Coming Out Fighting* (1969) and *Women and Animals* (1972).

JOHN HUGHES was born in Belfast in 1962 and educated at St Patrick's High School, Downpatrick, and Queen's University Belfast, where he took a degree in English. He has published four collections of poems: *The Something in Particular* (1986), *Negotiations With the Chill Wind* (1991), *The Devil Himself* (1996) and *Fast Forward* (2003).

TESS HURSON was born in 1955 in the townland of Annaghbeg on the Tyrone/Armagh border and educated at Trinity College Dublin, Queen's University Belfast and York University, Toronto. She wrote a doctoral thesis on the novels of Flann O'Brien and her publications include *Inside the Margin: A Carleton Reader*. Her collection of poems *Vivarium* was published in 1987.

PHILIP LARKIN (1922–85) was born in Coventry and educated at King Henry VIII School, Coventry, and St John's College, Oxford. In 1950 he was appointed sub-librarian at Queen's University Belfast, a post he held until 1955, when he became Librarian at the University of Hull. He was awarded an honorary degree by Queen's in 1969. Larkin's reputation as one of the most important English poets of the twentieth century is based on the four slim volumes he published during his lifetime: *The North Ship* (1945), *The Less Deceived* (1955), *The Whitsun Weddings* (1964) and *High Windows* (1974). He edited *The Oxford Book of Twentieth-Century English Verse* in 1973 and his *Collected Poems*, edited by Anthony Thwaite, appeared in 1988.

LAURENCE LERNER was born in Cape Town, South Africa, in 1925 and educated at the University of Cape Town and Pembroke College, Cambridge. He was employed as extra-mural tutor, then lecturer in English at Queen's University Belfast (1953–62). He was Professor of English at the University of Sussex, Brighton (1970–84), and at Vanderbilt University, Nashville, Tennessee from 1985. Among his collections of poetry are *Selected Poems* (1984) and *Rembrandt's Mirror* (1987).

MICHAEL LONGLEY was born in Belfast in 1939 and educated at the Royal Belfast Academical Institution and Trinity College Dublin, where he graduated in 1963 with a degree in Classics. He was Literature Officer and Traditional Arts Officer at the Arts Council of Northern Ireland from 1970–91. He attended the writers' group at Queen's throughout the 1960s and was one of the gifted group of Ulster poets who published their first books at the end of that decade. He was awarded an honorary degree by Queen's in 1995. His *Selected Poems* appeared in 1998 and his *Collected Poems* in 2006. He is married to the critic Edna Longley, Emeritus Professor of English at Queen's University Belfast.

LEON McAULEY was born in Dungannon, County Tyrone, in 1952 and educated at St MacNissi's College, Garron Tower, and Queen's University Belfast. He has worked as a teacher, printer, broadcaster and an Arts Council artist in the community, and his photographs have been exhibited throughout Northern Ireland. His collection of poems *Veronica* was published by Lagan Press in 1994.

ROY McFADDEN (1921–99) was born in Belfast and attended Regent House School and Queen's University Belfast, where he studied Law. He was a leading member of the group of Ulster poets who began to publish in book form in the 1940s. With Robert Greacen, he co-edited *Ulster Voices* (later *Irish Voices*) in 1943, was an editor of *Lagan* (1945–45) and founded and co-edited *Rann* (1948–53). He practised as a solicitor in Belfast until his retirement. His *Collected Poems 1943–1995* was published in 1996.

JOHN McGUCKIAN was born in Ballymena, County Antrim, in 1943 and educated at St MacNissi's College, Garron Tower, and Queen's University Belfast (1961–66) He has worked as a teacher in Preston, Stoke-on-Trent, Ballymena and Belfast and is married to the poet Medbh McGuckian. His collection of poems *Talking With My Brother* was published in 2002. He was awarded an MA in Creative Writing by Queen's in 2004.

MEDBH McGUCKIAN was born in Belfast in 1950 and educated at Dominican College, Fortwilliam, Belfast and Queen's University Belfast (1968–74). She was writer in residence at Queen's from 1986 to 1988 and has also worked as writer in residence at the University of Ulster and at Trinity College Dublin. She has, to date, published eleven collections of poems, including *Selected Poems* (1999) and, most recently, *Had I a Thousand Lives* (2003) and *The Book of the Angel* (2004).

GEARÓID MAC LOCHLAINN was born in Belfast in 1967 and educated at Queen's University Belfast. He has published two collections in the Irish language, *Babylon Gaeilgóir* (1997) and *Na Scéalaithe* (1999) and a bilingual selection of his work, *Scruth Teangacha/Stream of Tongues* (2002), with an introduction by Nuala Ni Dhomhnaill, which won the Michael Hartnett Award, the Butler Award and the Eithne and Rupert Strong Award. He has been employed as writer in residence at the University of Ulster and in the Department of Celtic and Irish Studies at Queen's.

GEORGE MCWHIRTER was born in Belfast in 1939 and educated at Boys' Model School, Grosvenor High School, Queen's University Belfast (1957–62) and the University of British Columbia, Vancouver. He taught in Ireland and elsewhere and was a professor and head of Creative Writing at the University of British Columbia (1983–93). He has been publishing poetry, novels, short stories and plays since 1971 and his poetry collections include *Queen of the Sea* (1976), *Fire before Dark* (1983) and *Incubus: The Dark Side of the Light* (1995).

TOM MATTHEWS (1945–2003) was born in Ballymena, County Antrim, in 1945 and brought up in Derry, where he was educated at Foyle College. He graduated from Queen's University Belfast and worked for a time as a chemist in a cement works in Larne, County Antrim. His collection *Dr Wilson as an Arab* was published in 1974.

MARTIN MOONEY was born in Belfast in 1964 and grew up in Newtownards, where he was educated at Regent House School. He graduated from Queen's University Belfast in 1986 with a degree in English and Philosophy. He has published three collections of poems: *Grub* (1993), *Rasputin and His Children* (2001, re-issued 2003) and *Blue Lamp Disco* (2003).

SINEAD MORRISSEY was born in Portadown, County Armagh, in 1972. She was educated at Belfast High School and Trinity

College Dublin and worked for several years abroad in Japan and
New Zealand before returning to Belfast in 1999. She was writer
in residence at Queen's University Belfast from 2002 to 2005 and
has published three collections of poems: *There Was Fire in
Vancouver* (1996), *Between Here and There* (2002) and *The State
of the Prisons* (2005).

PAUL MULDOON was born in County Armagh in 1951 and
educated at St Patrick's College, Armagh, and at Queen's
University Belfast (1969–73). He worked as a radio and television
producer for BBC Northern Ireland from 1973 to 1986. Since
1987 he has lived in the United States, where he is the Howard
G.B. Clark Professor in Humanities at Princeton University. In
1999 he became the Professor of Poetry at Oxford University. He
edited *The Faber Book of Contemporary Irish Poetry* in 1986. His
most recent collections of poems are *Poems 1968–1998* (2001),
*Moy Sand and Gravel* (2002), which won the Pulitzer Prize for
Poetry, and *Horse Latitudes* (2006).

JOAN NEWMANN was born in Tandragee, County Armagh, in 1942
and educated at Portadown Technical College, Rupert Stanley
College, Belfast, and as a mature student at Queen's University
Belfast, graduating in 1981. She had previously been a member of
Philip Hobsbaum's writers' group at the University. She lives with
her daughter Kate in County Donegal, where they run the
Summer Palace Press. Her collections of poems are *Coming of Age*
(1995) and *Thin Ice* (1998).

KATE NEWMANN, daughter of the poet Joan Newmann, was born
in County Down in 1965 and educated at Friends' School,
Lisburn, and King's College, Cambridge, where she read English.
She worked as a junior fellow at the Institute of Irish Studies at
Queen's, compiling *The Dictionary of Ulster Biography* (1993).
Her collection of poems *The Blind Woman in the Blue House* was
published in 2001.

GRÉAGÓIR Ó DÚILL was born in Dublin in 1946 and grew up in County Antrim, where he was educated at St Malachy's College, Belfast, and Queen's University Belfast (1964–68). Later he did postgraduate work in Irish at University College Dublin and Maynooth. He edited the magazine *Comhar* and a number of anthologies of poetry in Irish, most notably *Filíocht Uladh 1980–85* (1986) and *Fearann Pinn: Filíocht 1900–1999*. He has worked as a teacher and civil servant and was on the faculty of the Poets' House. His eight collections of poems in Irish include *Blaoscoilean* (1989), *Saothar an Ghoirt* (1994), *Garbh Achadh* (1996) and *An Fhuinneog Thuaidh* (2000). *Traverse*, a selection of his poems translated into English, was published in 1998 and a bi-lingual selection, *Gone to Earth*, in 2005. He has served as a visiting lecturer in the Department of Celtic and Irish Studies at Queen's.

PÓL Ó MUIRÍ was born in Belfast in 1965 and educated at Queen's University Belfast. In addition to *Flight from Shadow* (1995), a study of Seosamh MacGrianna, he has published several collections of poems in Irish. A volume of poetry in English, *D-Day*, was published in 1995.

FRANK ORMSBY was born in Enniskillen, County Fermanagh, in 1947 and educated at St Michael's College, Enniskillen, and Queen's University Belfast. He was editor of *The Honest Ulsterman* from 1969 to 1989 and has also edited a number of anthologies, including *Poets from the North of Ireland*, *A Rage for Order: Poetry of the Northern Ireland Troubles* and *The Hip Flask: Short Poems from Ireland*. He has published three collections of poetry – most recently *The Ghost Train* in 1995. He has been Head of English at the Royal Belfast Academical Institution since 1975.

CATHAL Ó SEARCAIGH was born in County Donegal in 1956 and educated at the National Institute of Higher Education, Limerick, and at Maynooth. He lived for a time in London, then Dublin, where he worked with RTÉ, before returning to Donegal. From 1992 to 1995 he served as Irish language writer in residence in the Department of Celtic Studies at Queen's University Belfast. He is one of the leading contemporary poets writing in Irish. Among his most recent collections of poems are *Na Buachailli Bana* (1996) and *Out in the Open* (2000), with English translations by Frank Sewell.

STEWART PARKER (1941–88) was born in Belfast and educated at Sullivan Upper School, Holywood, and Queen's University Belfast (1959–64), where he attended meetings of Philip Hobsbaum's writers' group, co-founded the magazine *Interest*, and helped form the New Stage Club. Though Parker published pamphlets of poems in the 1960s, he made his reputation as a writer of plays for radio, television and the stage. His poems were published in 2004 under the title *Paddy Dies*.

VICTOR PRICE was born in Newcastle, County Down, in 1930 and educated at Methodist College, Belfast, and Queen's University Belfast (1947–51), where he studied French and German. With H.A. Barrington, he founded *Q* magazine in 1950. He taught in Ireland and Germany and then worked in broadcasting in Belfast, Hong Kong and London. He has published three novels and translations of a number of plays by George Buchner. He also edited *Apollo in Mourne* (1978), a selection of Richard Rowley's poems, plays and stories. His volume of poems *Two Parts Water* appeared in 1980.

W.R. RODGERS (1909–69) was born in Belfast and was educated at Queen's, graduating in 1931 with a degree in English. In 1935 he was ordained and became Presbyterian minister at Loughgall, County Armagh. He left the ministry in 1946 and joined the BBC in London, living at various times in Essex and Suffolk. In 1966 he moved to Claremont, California, to take up a post as writer in residence at Pitzer College and later taught at California State Polytechnic College. He died in Los Angeles and is buried in

Loughgall. His *Collected Poems* appeared in 1971 and was re-issued in 1993, edited by Michael Longley.

CAROL RUMENS was born in London in 1944 and read Philosophy at London University. She has worked as an advertising copywriter, freelance reviewer and teacher of creative writing, with residencies at a number of universities, such as Kent, Newcastle, Durham and University College Cork. She was writer in residence at Queen's University Belfast from 1991 to 1994. She has edited several anthologies and her collections of poems include *Thinking of Skins: New and Selected Poems* (1993), *Best China Sky* (1995), *Holding Pattern* (1998) and *Poems 1968–2004* (2004).

JAMES SIMMONS (1933–2001), poet and singer/songwriter, was born in Derry and educated at Foyle College, Derry, Campbell College, Belfast, and Leeds University, where he graduated with a degree in English in 1958. He lectured in Nigeria and at the New University of Ulster (later the University of Ulster) at Coleraine. He founded *The Honest Ulsterman* magazine in 1968 and edited the first nineteen issues. From 1989 to 1992 he served as a writer in residence at Queen's University Belfast. In 1990 he and his wife, the American poet Janice Fitzpatrick, founded the Poets' House, which (in conjunction with the University of Lancaster) offered an MA in Creative Writing, the first degree of its kind in Ireland. His *Poems 1956–1986,* introduced by Edna Longley, was published in 1986 and re-issued in 2002.

JANICE FITZPATRICK SIMMONS was born in Boston in 1954 and grew up in Wellesley, Massachusetts, and Barrington, Rhode Island. In 1986 she was awarded an MA in English Literature by the University of New Hampshire. She worked as Assistant Director of the Frost Place in Franconia. She co-founded the Poets' House with her husband, the poet James Simmons, in 1990. She taught for a time in the Department of English at Queen's. Her three poetry collections are *Settler* (1995), *Starting at Purgatory* (1999) and *The Bowspirit* (2005).

G. SINGH was born in Jaipur, India, in 1926 and has degrees from the universities of Rasjasthan, Bologna and London. He was appointed lecturer in Italian at Queen's University Belfast in 1965 and was professor of Italian there from 1972 to 1992. He published a critical study of Eugenio Montale in 1973 and his translations of Montale's poetry appear in *Xenia* (1970) and *New Poems* (1976). He is also an expert on the Italian poet/philosopher Giacomo Leopardi and an authority on Ezra Pound and F.R. Leavis.

DAMIAN SMYTH was born in Downpatrick, County Down, in 1962. He holds a doctorate in contemporary philosophy from Queen's University Belfast and works as Literature Officer for the Arts Council of Northern Ireland. His play *Soldiers of the Queen* was staged in 2002 and he has published two collections of poems: *Downpatrick Races* (2000) and *The Down Recorder* (2004).

ARTHUR TERRY (1927–2004) was born in York and read Modern Languages at Cambridge (1944–47). He joined the staff of Queen's University Belfast in the 1950s and served as Professor of Spanish there from 1962 to 1972. He was a member of Philip Hobsbaum's writers' group and Festival Publications issued two pamphlets of his translations. His translations from the Catalan of Gabriel Ferrater were published in 2004 under the title *Women and Days*, with an introduction by Seamus Heaney.

HELEN WADDELL (1889–1965), scholar and translator, was born in Tokyo, where her father was a Presbyterian minister. She was educated at Victoria College, Belfast, Queen's University Belfast (1908–1912) and Somerville College, Oxford. Her best known works are *The Wandering Scholars* (1927), *The Desert Fathers* (1936), *Medieval Latin Lyrics* (1929) and the novel *Peter Abelard* (1933). She was the first woman fellow of the Royal Society of Literature and a founding member of the Irish Academy of Letters. She received an honorary degree from Queen's in 1934.

SABINE WICHERT was born in Graudenz, West Prussia (now Grudziadz, Poland) in 1942 and grew up in West Germany. She has taught History at Queen's University Belfast since 1971 and has published three collections of poems: *Tin Drum Country* (1995), *Sharing Darwin* (1999) and *Taganrog* (2004).

# ACKNOWLEDGEMENTS

GRATEFUL ACKNOWLEDGEMENT IS MADE TO

Arc Publications Ltd for permission to reprint the following poems by
Gabriel Ferrater: 'A Small War' and 'Time Was', translated by
Arthur Terry, from *Women and Days* (2004)

Black Mountain Press for permission to reprint the following poem by
Gréagóir Ó Dúill: 'Sionnach', translated by Bernie Kenny, from
*Gone to Earth* (2005)

Blackstaff Press for permission to reprint the following poem by
Joan Newmann: 'The Angel of Death' from *Coming of Age* (1995)

Blackstaff Press on behalf of the Estate of John Hewitt for permission to
reprint the following poems: 'The King's Horses' and 'Substance and
Shadow' from *The Collected John Hewitt* (1991)

Bloodaxe Books for permission to reprint the following poems by
Carol Rumens: 'Prayer for Northern Ireland' and 'Stealing the Genre'
from *Poems 1968–2004* (2004)

Carcanet Press Ltd for permission to reprint the following poems by
Sinead Morrissey: 'Clocks' from *The State of the Prisons* (2005) and
'Sea Stones' from *Between Here and There* (2002)

Cló Iar-Connachta for permission to reprint the following poems by
Cathal Ó Searcaigh: 'Do Isaac Rosenberg', translated by Frank Sewell,
from *Out in the Open* (1997) and 'I gCeann Mo Thrí Bliana A
Bhí Mé' from *Homecoming/An Bealach 'na Bhaile*; for permission to
reprint the following poem by Gearóid Mac Lochlainn: 'An Máine
Gaelach', translated by Ciaran Carson, from *Sruth Teangacha/Stream
of Tongues* (2002)

Dedalus Press for permission to reprint the following poem by
Chris Agee: 'Mushrooming' from *In the New Hampshire Woods* (1992)

Andrew Elliot for permission to reprint the following poem: 'Angel'
from *The Creationists* (1988)

Faber and Faber Ltd for permission to reprint the following poems by
Paul Muldoon: 'The Green Gown' and 'Truce' from *Poems 1968–1998*

The Estate of Philip Hobsbaum for permission to reprint 'The Astigmatic' from *In Retreat and Other Poems* (1966) and 'Girl Reporter' from *The Place's Fault and Other Poems* (1964)

Lagan Press and the author for permission to reprint the following poem by Jean Bleakney: 'By Starlight on Narin Strand' from *The Ripple Tank Experiment* (1999); for permission to reprint the following poem by John Campbell: 'An Oul Jobbin' Poet' from *The Rose and the Blade* (2005); for permission to reprint the following poem by Deirdre Cartmill: 'The Waterfall Walk' from *Midnight Solo* (2004); for permission to reprint the following poem by C.L. Dallat: 'Morning Star' from *Morning Star* (1998); for permission to reprint the following poem by Moyra Donaldson: 'Words from the Other Side' from *Beneath the Ice* (2001); for permission to reprint the following poem by James Ellis: 'Over the Bridge' from *Domestic Flight* (1998); for permission to reprint the following poem by Janice Fiztpatrick Simmons: 'Salt Caress' from *The Bowspirit* (2005); for permission to reprint the following poems by Robert Greacen: 'Carnival by the River' and 'St Andrew's Day' from *Collected Poems 1943–1995*; for permission to reprint the following poem by Tess Hurson: 'Rite of Spring' from *Vivarium* (1997); for permission to reprint the following poem by Leon McAuley: 'The Children of Lir' from *Veronica* (1994); for permission to reprint the following poem by Martin Mooney: 'Footballers in the Snow' from *Rasputin and his Children* (2003); for permission to reprint the following poem by Pól Ó Muirí: 'Bobby, Wilfred and Seán' from *D-Day* (1995); for permission to reprint the following poem by Damian Smyth: 'Disappeared' from *Downpatrick Races* (2000); for permission to reprint the following poem by Sabine Wichert: 'The Smell of Frying Cheese' from *Taganrog* (2004)

Lagan Press and the author's Estate for permission to reprint the following poem by Mairtín Crawford: 'Untitled Sonnet' from *Selected Poems* (2005)

Lagan Press and the family of Roy McFadden for permission to reprint the following poems: 'The Hunger-marchers' and 'My Mother's Young Sister' from *Collected Poems 1943–1995* (1996)

Laurence Lerner for permission to reprint the following poems: 'Raspberries' and 'In Memoriam' from *Selected Poems* (1984)

Michael Longley for permission to reprint the following poem: 'The Leveret'

148

George McWhirter for permission to reprint the following poem: 'Homework' from *Fire Before Dark* (Oberon, 1983)

The Estate of Tom Matthews for permission to reprint 'Robert Sat' from *Dr Wilson as an Arab* (1974)

The Marvell Press, England and Australia, for permission to reprint the following poems by Philip Larkin: 'Church Going' and 'Reasons for Attendance' from *The Less Deceived* (1955)

Frank Ormsby for permission to reprint the following poem: 'One Looks at One'

Peterloo Poets for permission to reprint the following poem by Victor Price: 'Jeanie' from *Two Parts Water* (1980)

G. Singh for permission to reprint the following poems: 'In the Smoke' from *New Poems* (1976); 'The Carillon Pendulum Clock' from *It Depends: A Poet's Notebook* (1980)

Summer Palace Press for permission to reprint the following poem by Ruth Carr: 'The Blue Bowl' from *There is a House* (2004); for permission to reprint the following poem by John McGuckian: 'Irish Hare' from *Talking with My Brother* (2002); for permission to reprint the following poem by Kate Newmann: 'Dream of a Portrait Painter on a Sunday Afternoon in the Alameda' from *The Blind Woman in the Blue House*; for permission to reprint the following poem by Stewart Parker: 'Paddy Dies' from *Paddy Dies* (2004)

The Estate of Helen Waddell for permission to reprint the following poems: 'Epitaph for his Niece, Sophia' and 'Lament for Hathimoda, Abbess of Gandesheim' from *More Latin Lyrics* (1976)


Every effort has been made to trace and contact copyright holders before publication. If notified, the publisher will rectify any errors or omissions at the earliest opportunity.

# INDEX OF TITLES

First published in 2006 by
Blackstaff Press
4c Heron Wharf, Sydenham Business Park
Belfast BT3 9LE, Northern Ireland

in association with
Queen's University Belfast

Queen's University
Belfast

The Acknowledgements on pp. 146–9
constitute an extension of this copyright page.

Designed by Dunbar Design
Printed in Northern Ireland by Nicholson & Bass

A CIP catalogue record for this book
is available from the British Library

ISBN PAPERBACK 0-85640-796-8
ISBN HARDBACK 0-85640-797-6
ISBN FINE EDITION 0-85640-798-4

www.blackstaffpress.com
www.qub.ac.uk
www.qub.ac.uk/heaneycentre